Digital Information Technology

Pearson BTEC Level 1/2 Tech Award

Component 3

P.M. Heathcote and

A. Weidmann

Published by
PG Online Limited
The Old Coach House
35 Main Road
Tolpuddle
Dorset
DT2 7EW
United Kingdom
sales@pgonline.co.uk
www.pgonline.co.uk
2019

PG ONLINE

Pearson Endorsement Statement

In order to ensure that this resource offers high-quality support for the associated Pearson qualification, it has been through a review process by the awarding body. This process confirms that this resource fully covers the teaching and learning content of the specification or part of a specification at which it is aimed. It also confirms that it demonstrates an appropriate balance between the development of subject skills, knowledge and understanding, in addition to preparation for assessment.

Endorsement does not cover any guidance on assessment activities or processes (e.g. practice questions or advice on how to answer assessment questions), included in the resource nor does it prescribe any particular approach to the teaching or delivery of a related course.

While the publishers have made every attempt to ensure that advice on the qualification and its assessment is accurate, the official specification and associated assessment guidance materials are the only authoritative source of information and should always be referred to for definitive guidance.

Pearson examiners have not contributed to any sections in this resource relevant to examination papers for which they have responsibility.

Examiners will not use endorsed resources as a source of material for any assessment set by Pearson. Endorsement of a resource does not mean that the resource is required to achieve this Pearson qualification, nor does it mean that it is the only suitable material available to support the qualification, and any resource lists produced by the awarding body shall include this and other appropriate resources.

Acknowledgements

Every effort has been made to trace and acknowledge ownership of copyright. The publishers will be happy to make any future amendments with copyright owners. The author and publisher would like to thank the following companies and individuals who granted permission for the use of their images in this textbook.

Chapter 2
Google data centre: © Rudmer Zwerver / Shutterstock.com
Dropbox app and website: © Nopparat Khokthong / Shutterstock.com
Spotify website: © Casimiro PT / Shutterstock.com

Chapter 4
Amazon headquarters: © Ken Wolter / Shutterstock.com

Chapter 5
Posters Do's and don'ts of designing for users with accessibility needs © Open Government Licence

Chapter 7
British Airways aeroplane: © Rebius / Shutterstock.com

Chapter 8
BitTorrent screen: © pixinoo / Shutterstock.com
Apple headquarters: © Droneandy / Shutterstock.com
Facebook screen: © hafakot / Shutterstock.com

Chapter 9
Minister Ursula von der Leyen © Alexandros Michailidis / Shutterstock.com

Chapter 12
Dirk supermarket checkout: © Robert Hoetink / Shutterstock.com
Worker disassembling a printer: © Creatikon Studio / Shutterstock.com

Chapter 14
Johannesburg classroom © Rich T Photo / Shutterstock.com

Chapter 15
Social media icons © tanuha2001 / Shutterstock.com
Linkedin homepage: © JuliusKielaitis / Shutterstock.com

Chapter 16
Batchelors logo: © chrisdorney / Shutterstock.com
Creative Commons webpage: © Casimiro PT / Shutterstock.com

Chapter 17
Santander sign: © Alf Ribeiro / Shutterstock.com

Chapter 20
Oyster card terminal: © dennizn / Shutterstock.com

Preface

This book provides comprehensive coverage of the externally assessed Component 3 (Effective Digital Working Practices) specification. It is designed to be used both as an interactive text in the classroom, and as an individual student revision aid.

In-text questions in every chapter challenge the students to think about what they are learning, do further research and formulate answers which can then be discussed in class. End-of-chapter exercises, using command words such as State, Describe, Explain and Discuss, that students may encounter in an exam, may be set as homework. These exercises give students invaluable insight and experience in writing the types of answers which will gain full marks in the final exam. Solutions to all questions and exercises are provided in a free teacher pack available to teachers only on our website www.pgonline.co.uk.

The four sections of the book correspond to Learning Aims A to D of the BTEC specification. To accompany this textbook, PG Online also publishes a series of four downloadable teaching units. Each topic in a unit consists of a PowerPoint presentation, teacher's notes, worksheets, homework sheets and a final assessment with practice examination-style questions.

First edition 2019

A catalogue entry for this book is available from the British Library

ISBN: 978-1-910523-14-8

Copyright © PM Heathcote and A Weidmann 2019

All rights reserved

Printed and bound in Great Britain by Bell & Bain Limited

Contents

Pearson BTEC

Component 3: Effective Digital Working Practices

		Pack A	Pack B	Pack C	Pack D
Learning Aim A: Modern technologies					
A1	Modern technologies	✓			
A2	Impact of modern technologies	✓			
Learning Aim B: Cyber security					
B1	Threats to data		✓		
B2	Prevention and management of threats to data		✓		
B3	Policy		✓		
Learning Aim C: The wider implications of digital systems					
C1	Responsible use			✓	
C2	Legal and ethical			✓	
Learning Aim D: Planning and communication in digital systems					
D1	Forms of notation				✓

Modern technologies

In this section:

Chapter 1
Communication technologies

Objectives

- Describe:
  - o setting up and using ad hoc networks
  - o security issues with open networks
  - o performance issues with ad hoc networks
  - o issues affecting network availability

Wi-Fi and cell networks

There are two major types of wireless Internet access. **Cell networks** cover more than 97% of the population in the UK, although the connection may be poor or non-existent inside a building, near tall city buildings or in rural locations.

 Q1 Suggest reasons why it may not be possible to get a mobile signal in a rural location.

Wi-Fi reception is available within a **Wi-Fi hotspot**, built into most mobile devices and into the wireless **router** commonly used at home or in a small office.

Setting up and using ad hoc networks

An **ad hoc network** is a temporary connection between two or more computing devices. For example, in ad hoc mode you can set up a wireless connection between your mobile phone and a laptop computer, or between a laptop and a PC.

For a more secure, wired connection, you can use a USB or ethernet cable to connect a laptop to the PC and configure settings on each computer.

Ad hoc networks are useful when you need to share files containing data or images with another computer. A laptop can also be connected to the Internet via a PC. If the PC has access to a Wi-Fi network through a router or wireless access point, one or more computers connected to this PC can share the Internet connection once the settings are correctly configured.

Tethering

Many office workers who commute daily by train use the journey to work on their laptops. Suppose Philip, a regular commuter, needs to connect to the Internet, for example to send an email. He cannot do this directly unless the train has a reliable Wi-Fi connection.

Instead, Philip can activate a **personal hotspot** function on his mobile phone by **tethering** it to the laptop via a cable or bluetooth. This is also a type of ad hoc network. Effectively, he is using his mobile phone as a wireless router to provide an Internet connection.

A window opens on his laptop to show all the mobile phone network connections nearby. Philip selects his phone from the list and types in his password.

The mobile phone uses the **cell network** to connect to the Internet. Philip is able to connect his laptop to the Internet by logging on to his mobile and using the cell network to create a **mobile hotspot**.

Performance issues with ad hoc networks

There are some disadvantages to using a personal (mobile) hotspot:

- Using a mobile hotspot drains the phone battery much faster than usual

- It may use up the monthly data limit

- The connection may not be as fast as using a standard Wi-Fi network. Ad hoc mode networks support 11 Mbps connection speeds, whereas standard Wi-Fi supports 54 Mbps or higher.

- Security is an issue when transmitting over an open network. Many people use a virtual private network (VPN) to encrypt and transmit their data securely (see overleaf).

- It is not possible to monitor signal strength, which means that maintaining a stable connection can be difficult, especially when the ad hoc devices change their positions, as for example on a train.

Virtual private network

A **virtual private network (VPN)** offers a higher degree of protection and privacy as you're surfing the web, whether at home or outside. A VPN creates a secure connection over public networks (such as the Wi-Fi in public transport, hotels or cafés) as well as home networks. By routing your traffic through specialised servers and encrypting your data, VPNs hide your online activity and protect you from hacker attacks, identity theft, and other criminal activity.

Issues affecting network availability

There are just four mobile (cell) network providers in the UK: EE, O2, Three and Vodafone. Each of these holds a licence to build and maintain their own mobile network infrastructure.

Each of the network providers covers 98-99% of the country. In some places, although there may be outdoor coverage, there may be no 3G or 4G coverage inside a building.

A cell site or cell tower holds the electronic equipment such as transmitters, receivers and antennae to create a cell in a cellular network. In rural areas, cell towers may be few and far between so coverage will be patchy.

A cell tower is typically 100-200ft high with a range of between 22 and 45 miles. Although it does not need a clear 'line of sight', radio interference can affect reception. The range of a cell tower is affected by:

- Geographical factors such as hills and valleys
- The height of the antenna over the surrounding landscape
- The power of the transmitter
- Buildings or vegetation in the vicinity

Some areas are **blackspots** where no mobile signal is available because of geographical features or buildings which block the signal.

> **Q2** Suggest reasons why a commuter who has set up an ad hoc network using her phone and laptop may sometimes lose the connection to the Internet.

Mobile coverage in cities

According to a 2017 survey, Middlesbrough was the best place in the UK to get 4G coverage at 82.7%, and Bournemouth was the worst with 67.5% coverage. London was also in the bottom five with 73.6% coverage.

Mobile cellular network antenna on a mast in a city

Mobile phone networks use microwaves to transmit signals. These microwaves spread well in free space, but not over very long distances, through walls or thick barriers, and very poorly around corners.

In cities, there are a vast number of surfaces that can reflect, absorb or scatter microwave transmissions. Large buildings, often made of reflective materials, can create **dead zones** or **blackspots** where microwaves are blocked.

Open Wi-Fi

A wireless local area network (LAN) uses radio waves to connect devices such as laptops and mobile phones to the Internet, typically through a **wireless router**. **Wireless access points**, also known as **wireless hotspots**, are found in public locations and provide Internet access to a mobile phone or laptop when you are away from home or office. When you connect to a Wi-Fi hotspot in a cafe, hotel, airport lounge or other public place, you're connecting to that business's wireless network. You may need to ask for a password to sign on to the network.

Security issues with open networks

Open networks do not encrypt data while it is being transmitted, and a hacker could intercept the data. You could be sharing a connection with anyone. You should never use an open network - particularly to make an online purchase, connect to your bank account or enter personal details. Personal information, account or credit card details could be stolen and used fraudulently. Many people have started to use private VPNs to ensure the security of their transmissions.

Network availability in developing countries

Mobile phones have transformed communications in developing countries. Landline infrastructure is very expensive to install, and telephone cables are likely to be damaged or stolen. However, it is relatively fast and inexpensive to set up a single cell tower that can connect multiple villages wirelessly. Satellites are commonly used to connect the towers to the main hub, which may be hundreds of miles away.

Virtually no country in the world now has no mobile coverage. However, in 35 countries including India, Indonesia, Ghana and Ethiopia, less than 20% of the population has Internet access.

Exercises

1. Amy is on holiday in the country. She wants to contact her friends on social media but there is no mobile signal in the house she is staying in. She goes to a local café which advertises a Wi-Fi connection.

   (a) Give **two** possible reasons why she cannot get a mobile signal in the house. [2]

   (b) Describe **one** way in which she can connect to the Internet using the café's Wi-Fi connection. [2]

   (c) Explain **one** security issue associated with using the network provided by the café. [2]

   (d) State **one** performance issue associated with using the network provided by the café. [1]

2. Ewan is travelling to work by train. There is no Wi-Fi connection and Ewan needs to connect his laptop to the Internet so that he can download some images for a report he is working on.

   (a) Describe how he can use his mobile to set up an ad hoc network to access the Internet. [4]

   (b) Occasionally Ewan loses the signal and the Internet connection is dropped.
   Give **one** reason why this might happen. [2]

   (c) Describe **two** other issues that may influence Ewan's decision to use an ad hoc network. [4]

3. This question is about telephone communication.

   (a) Describe **two** issues affecting cell network availability in the UK. [4]

   (b) Describe **one** reason why telephone communication in developing countries has improved over the past few years. [2]

Chapter 2
Cloud storage and cloud computing

Objectives

- Describe features and uses of cloud storage:
  - setting and sharing of access rights, synchronisation of cloud and individual devices, availability (24/7), scalability

- Describe features and uses of cloud computing:
  - online applications, consistency of versions between users, single shared instance of a file, collaboration tools/features

- Describe how the selection of platforms and services impacts on the use of cloud technologies:
  - number and complexity of features, paid for vs free, interface design, available devices

What is cloud storage?

Traditionally, all files containing data were stored on an individual's PC or on a network **file server**. It is now common for both organisations and individuals to sign up for an Internet file storage service such as Dropbox, Microsoft OneDrive or Google Cloud.

A storage facility owned and maintained by a third party, accessed via the Internet, is referred to as **cloud storage**.

A Google data centre

Cloud storage facilities consist of hundreds of high-capacity hard disk or solid-state drives housed in a building and kept running continuously. Google has dozens of data centres scattered around the world, with at least 12 major storage facilities in the US and others across Asia and Europe.

Using cloud storage

Anyone using an Internet-based email provider such as Gmail or social media is already using cloud storage.

If you want to store your data (including images, videos or other files) in the cloud, a provider such as Dropbox will give you a free monthly allowance of say 2GB of space, after which you pay according to the amount of data you store. You can download free apps to access cloud storage from your computer, phone or tablet, via the Internet.

 Describe some cloud storage or cloud applications that you use.

Setting and sharing of access rights

When you set up an account with a cloud storage provider, you can specify that selected other people (identified by their email accounts) can share particular folders. You can add, change or delete other people's access rights to your account whenever you like.

Synchronisation of cloud and individual devices

Any time you create or edit a file and save it to Dropbox, for example, it will also be saved on the device that you created it on. The cloud storage software will automatically synchronise with Dropbox and you can access the new version from your phone.

To sync across your computers, phones, and tablets:

1. Install the cloud storage app on all computers, phones, and tablets you want to sync with.
2. Sign in to the same cloud storage account on each computer, phone, and tablet.
3. Add files into your cloud storage folder. As long as a file is in your cloud storage folder, it syncs to all your connected computers, phones, and tablets.

Your devices can all access the same cloud storage account. Once you sign in, you have access to your cloud storage files, no matter where you are.

 Explain why someone using a laptop in a restaurant may need to have their smartphone nearby in order to access the Internet.

Advantages of cloud storage

- All files are kept backed up in the cloud, so you will never lose a file. Files deleted accidentally can be retrieved.
- You can access your files from any of your computing devices with an Internet connection.
- You can access your files from anywhere in the world.
- You can share files with friends or colleagues and they can update or add files to your shared folders, at any time of day or night (24/7), provided they have an Internet connection.
- You pay only for the amount of storage you need. If you need only a small amount, it may be free.

Cloud computing

As well as storing data files in the cloud, you can use software that is held in the cloud, rather than on your own computer or on a network file server.

Using software such as Google Docs:

- Several people can work together on the same document at the same time, creating a **single, consistent version.** You don't end up with several different versions of the same file.
- All the changes are saved automatically in real time as you type.
- **Collaboration tools** enable you to chat and comment while you are working on a document with someone else.
- If you need to see what changes have been made since you last worked on a document, you can use revision history to see old versions of the same document, sorted by date and who made the changes.

Cloud computing in business

Both individuals and organisations use numerous different software applications held in the cloud. This is known as **Software as a Service**, or **SaaS**.

Using **accounting software**, for example, authorised employees in the company can view the business accounts, or add new transactions, from wherever they are. All the files will be updated immediately.

- An accountant working in a remote office can view and audit the accounts
- A sales person visiting another company can enter details of a sale
- An accounts manager in the office can use the software to prepare a budget for the next year

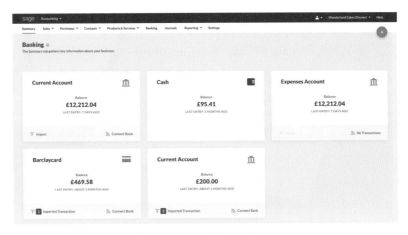

Sage accounting software

Computing platforms

A **platform** is the term used to describe the combination of hardware and operating system being used for a particular application. Here are some examples of platforms:

- A PC running the Windows 10 operating system
- An Apple Macbook (laptop computer) running the macOS operating system
- A Samsung smartphone running the Android operating system
- An Apple iPhone7 running the iOS7 operating system
- An Amazon Fire tablet using an Android-based mobile operating system
- A Raspberry Pi running the Linux operating system

Websites

An organisation needing a website will generally use a **web provider** to host the website. The in-house designers may design and create the website, including the interface with menus, navigation links, content and so on. Alternatively, they may ask a specialised **third-party** organisation to design it for them.

Either way, when the website is up and running, it is hosted on the Internet, or to put it another way, in the **cloud**. This means that any time you use a website to order goods, renew a library book or reserve a seat on a train, for example, you are using cloud technology.

Selecting platforms and services

Suppose you want to sign up for a music streaming service so that you can download music to your PC or mobile phone whenever you want. Your choice of streaming service may depend on a number of factors.

Paid for versus free

Free versions of many cloud applications are available to the user, paid for by advertisements in either still, video or audio form played at regular intervals. A monthly subscription may have to be paid for an advert-free version.

Some services have a family option which allows several family members to sign up for a slightly increased monthly premium.

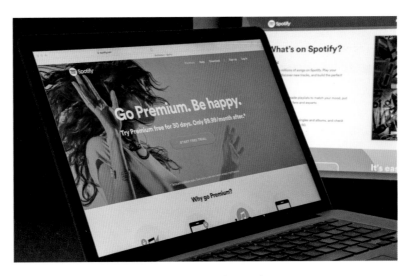

Spotify music streaming software

Number and complexity of features

The software may have additional features like playlists, recently played items, favourites and suggestions. You may be able to create libraries of songs and albums. Some streaming services may offer live programming or display song lyrics so that you can sing along. Some may also have better sound quality than others.

Interface design

- The interface **design** and **layout** will influence how easy the service is to find the music you want to play.
- Accessibility features may enable a user with a disability to use the site. For example, spoken instructions may enable a blind or partially sighted person to use the service.
- The service needs to be available on different platforms, for example a PC, tablet and mobile phone.

Exercises

1. BetterBake is a small online retailer selling kitchen tools and utensils. Their office computers are connected in a local area network with a file server which stores their company data. The file server's hard disk is almost full.

   The management has decided to move to cloud storage.

   (a) Describe what is meant by cloud storage. [2]

   (b) Explain **three** advantages to BetterBake of using cloud storage. [6]

   (c) Betterbake's management has decided to invest in cloud software which will enable members of a team putting together their next catalogue to work together on the document at the same time.

   Describe **two** facilities of the software which enable this type of collaboration. [4]

   (d) The BetterBake website is currently hosted on the company's web server. They have experienced problems on some occasions and have decided to engage a web provider to create and host a new website in the cloud.

   Describe **two** possible problems, apart from disk storage space, that will be overcome by having the website hosted by a web provider. [4]

2. Joanne wants to sign up for a music streaming service. She needs the ability to download and save music on her device.

   (a) Explain **three** other factors she should take into account when choosing a streaming service. [6]

   (b) Zena pays a monthly subscription to a music streaming service.

   One of the features the service offers is the ability to download and save music on her device.

   Explain **two** reasons why Zena may find this feature useful. [4]

Chapter 3
Using cloud technologies

Objectives

- Describe how cloud and traditional systems are used together
  - device synchronisation, online/offline working, notifications

- Consider the implications for organisations when choosing cloud technologies:
  - disaster recovery policies, security of data, compatibility, maintenance, getting a service/storage up and running quickly, performance considerations

What is cloud computing?

Here is a brief recap of the essential features of cloud computing.

- Computing resources are on-demand and self-service. Using a simple interface, you can get all the processing power, storage and network that you need.

- These resources are accessible from anywhere over the Internet.

- The cloud service provider has a large pool of resources and allocates them to customers. This allows the provider to benefit from economies of scale and pass the savings on to the customer.

- Customers don't need to know the location of the resources; they could be anywhere in the world.

- If a customer needs more resources, they are immediately available. If fewer resources are needed, the customer can scale back; they pay only for what they use or reserve. If they stop using resources, they stop paying.

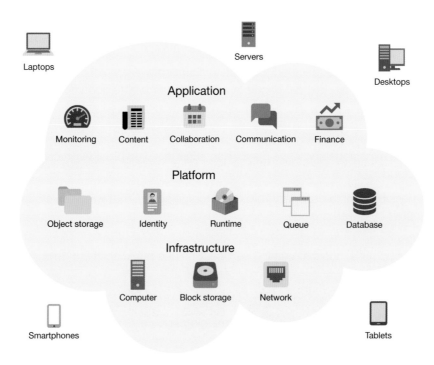

Cloud computing

Using cloud and traditional systems together

Some software providers offer both a cloud version and an offline version. For example, a free version of Microsoft Teams offers chat, video calling, files and apps which can be accessed online. Documents can be written, reviewed and co-authored online in real time. It is also possible to move from Office Online to the full-featured desktop version without leaving the document.

This enables a magazine editor, for example, to work with different contributors on articles they have created. When they are agreed on the content of an article, the editor can save it offline and work on it using the extra features provided by the desktop version of the word-processing software.

Device synchronisation

When you use a desktop application to save a file in shared cloud storage, the software will automatically synchronise the changes made on your computer to all connected devices. Files that are not in the cloud storage folders will not be synced to any other devices belonging to you or anyone else.

Online/offline working

In some organisations, many workers are not necessarily in the office every day. They may work in another geographically remote office, at home, or while travelling.

If the office network is down for any reason, or a Wi-Fi signal is not available, any files can still be saved in a shared area. They will not be saved immediately in the cloud, but copies of files are also saved offline on the user's device. When Internet access again becomes available, the files will be automatically synced.

Notifications

Cloud systems will send you notifications based on your activity, or what team members with shared access to the same folders are working on.

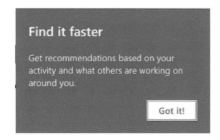

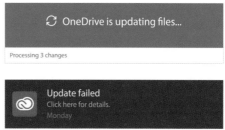

You can also display the current status of files in a shared area to see whether you have the most up-to-date version of a particular file, or whether the software is still syncing.

Notifications on mobile phones are also used to deliver real-time information to customers, often by email. These can be automatically generated messages such as billing information, scheduled reminders, news flashes or promotional advertisements. The user is notified by an audible sound, so the user does not have to keep checking their phone to see if there are any notifications which need attention.

On the other hand, they can arrive at inappropriate times and the interruptions can be very annoying.

Implications for organisations when choosing cloud technologies

Security of data

A survey of 1,400 IT decision-makers who use cloud services, carried out by McAfee™ in 2018, found that:

- 97% of all organisations use cloud services
- more than half the professionals surveyed traced a malware infection back to a cloud application
- one in four had experienced theft from the public cloud
- one in five had experienced an advanced attack against their public cloud infrastructure

In spite of these statistics, the great majority of organisations trust the cloud and realise the benefits of cloud security. Cloud providers look after security of data stored on their devices, but organisations have to be careful of what they put in the cloud, especially if it involves personal data about their clients or customers.

It is important to remember that data held on local servers and individual computers is also at risk. It is possible that some of the malware traced to the cloud was attached to files at the time they were saved to the cloud.

Data held by a cloud service provider is almost always stored in an encrypted form. This means it cannot be read by an intruder even if they are able to hack into it.

Backups are the responsibility of the cloud provider. This means it is not essential to back up data held on a local server or PC in real time or at the end of every day. Even if you accidentally delete data it can normally be recovered up to three months later from cloud storage. Cloud service providers back up data to additional remote servers so that it is almost guaranteed that they will never lose any of your data in the event of a catastrophe such as a fire or earthquake at one of their data centres.

Q1 **Do you think data is more secure saved in the cloud, or on your own computer? Give reasons for your answer.**

Disaster recovery

Planning for a disaster is an essential part of an organisation's IT department.

Risks which would have a severe impact on the ability to continue functioning normally might include:

- loss of access to premises
- loss of data
- loss of software and IT function
- loss of employees/skills

Recovery after a natural disaster such as fire, flood or earthquake will be much simpler if all of an organisation's data is held in the cloud. It may be necessary to:

- move premises temporarily or permanently
- to buy or hire new hardware

However, software and data can easily be restored from the cloud. This topic is covered in more detail in Chapter 11.

Compatibility

The choice of cloud software will depend to some extent on compatibility with existing systems. If it needs to integrate with an existing system that will be an important consideration.

Maintenance

System maintenance will be less complex.

- Software updates will be automatically installed by the cloud service provider with no action required by the user.
- Fewer staff and less expertise are required by an organisation to manage applications.
- There will be less downtime; updates installed by a cloud service provider are usually done out of office hours, for example at 2am when very few workers will be using the software.

 Describe some of the advantages for you of using cloud storage for photographs that you take, instead of saving them on your own personal device.

Getting a service or storage facility up and running quickly

Getting started with a cloud storage facility or cloud service provider is far easier, less time-consuming and less stressful, than installing a new server. There are companies that can help ensure a smooth changeover if needed.

Performance considerations

The first essential for using cloud storage or computing is a **fast broadband connection**. Without this, the responsiveness to user requests and synchronisation of devices may be slow. Uploading large files may take hours rather than minutes or seconds.

The management must ensure that the service or storage satisfies all the requirements of the organisation. It may need to be scalable, not only in volume but also in complexity. For example, an accounting package suitable for a company with a turnover of a few hundred thousand pounds may not fulfil needs when the turnover increases to several million pounds.

The software must be **responsive to users**; it may not run as fast as software installed on a local server, especially at busy periods of the day. Having to wait for the software to respond may affect employees' performance.

The organisation will need to ensure that the proposed cloud software will run on any of the **devices** that are used by employees.

Exercises

1. Mughal is the IT manager at HKL Ltd, a furniture manufacturer. One of his jobs is to carry out an assessment of risks to the data and software owned by the company.

    (a) Give **two** events which could have a severe impact on the IT department's ability to continue functioning normally.   [2]

    (b) Loss of data may be one result of a catastrophic event.

         Explain how the use of cloud storage can lessen the risks of data loss.   [2]

    (c) Explain **one** way in which cloud storage providers can ensure that, if the data in their storage facility is hacked, the hacker will not be able to make use of the data.   [2]

2. Gemma is the Managing Director of a small, rapidly growing company. The number of employees has doubled over the past year from ten to twenty. Disk storage space on the network server is running out.

    She has been investigating the advantages of moving to cloud storage and cloud computing.

    (a) Describe what is meant by cloud storage.   [3]

    (b) Describe what is meant by cloud computing.   [3]

    (c) Explain **two** ways in which moving to cloud storage could save money on hardware costs.   [4]

    (d) Explain **two** ways in which moving to cloud computing could save money on employee costs.   [4]

Chapter 4
Modern teams and modern technologies

Objectives

- Describe changes to modern teams facilitated by modern technologies:
  - based worldwide, multicultural, inclusive, in different time zones, flexible

- Describe how modern technologies can be used to manage modern teams:
  - collaboration tools, communication tools, scheduling and planning tools

- Describe how organisations use modern technologies to communicate with stakeholders
  - communication platforms (website, social media, email, voice communication)
  - selection of appropriate communication channels for sharing information, data and media

World teams

Organisations in many different fields, for example technology, science and business do not always operate solely in their home countries. They have a global market, and they need offices or shops in many different cities around the world in order to fully understand local culture and local needs, and to sell in different countries.

Amazon is based in Seattle, Washington. It has separate retail websites for almost 20 different countries translated into most major languages from English, French and Spanish to Chinese, Japanese and Turkish. It has 613,000 employees around the world.

Changes to modern teams facilitated by modern technologies

Modern technology has facilitated changes to modern teams in different ways.

- **World teams**: internal communication by email, conference calls, video calls, messaging and online chat enables team members to keep in regular communication.

- Team members may be based anywhere in the world, which means that the best mix of talents and diversity can be represented.

- Although people may work in different **time zones**, an email sent from the UK to someone in Australia can easily be responded to by early the next working day. This is a good alternative to a phone call to someone in a different time zone with a large time difference.

- Members of a team working in their own countries will be familiar with cultural norms, local holidays and customs based around religious festivals, and will be able to inform members at a head office based in London, for example, about **multicultural issues**.
- Technology has enabled **inclusivity**, so that people with a disability such as a deaf, blind or partially-sighted person, or someone with limited arm movement, can fully participate in a team with the use of specially-adapted computer equipment.
- **Flexible working** has been made possible. Team members may not necessarily need to come into the office every day; they can work at home using communication and cloud technologies. They will, to a certain extent, be able to have flexible working hours which fit in with family demands, taking children to school and picking them up, attending doctor's or dentist's appointments and so on.

Using technology to manage teams

Collaboration software is designed to help people working in a team to achieve their common goals.

Collaboration tools

Cloud software such as Google Docs (discussed in Chapter 2) enables many people to work together on a single document.

Cloud storage enables all users to access files that they need from anywhere at any time.

Scheduling tools

Calendar tools can be used to keep up-to-date with everyone's schedule from any location.

- Web-based cloud systems allow users to access and edit their calendars from any device, anywhere.
- Automatic emails and text reminders for events can be sent to individuals and group members.
- Events can be customised with icons, colours, links and notes.
- Share groups can include an unlimited number of users.
- Calendars of different users can be overlaid or viewed side by side so that different schedules can be easily compared.

Communication tools

Email, instant messaging, texting and online chat are all **communication tools**.

- Emails can be sent to many people simultaneously to keep everyone informed.
- Replies can be sent to all recipients of the original email, or just to the sender.
- Files can be attached to emails.
- A screenshot showing a sample layout, image or problem can be included in an email.
- Helpdesk workers can use software to view and control a user's screen to remotely solve a problem or adjust settings.
- Helpdesk workers may use online chat to suggest solutions to users' problems.
- Automatic translation software can be used for communications to team members working in different countries. A local content editor can check the accuracy of the translation before the email is sent.

Q1 **Describe ways in which you could use technology to work in a small team on a school project.**

Planning tools

Planning software is used to ensure that everyone in a team knows what stage each project task is at, who is responsible for the task, and what the schedule is. In some software, each task is assigned a 'card'. When part of a task is completed, this is recorded on the card and the card is moved to the next column in the planner. When the task reaches a 'completed' status, it is hidden on the planner.

Other software enables each team member to comment on the current status of their particular task in a project.

This week	Owner	Progress	Timeline	Hours	Priority
Issue new contracts	👤	Complete	March 2–15	7	High
Release new ad campaign	👤	Issues	March 4–11	10	Low
Contact clients	👤	In progress	March 11–23	8	High
Website design	👤	Complete	March 2–9	4	Low

Communicating with stakeholders

A **stakeholder** is anyone who is affected by or who can affect an organisation's actions and policies. Key stakeholders may include employees, shareholders, customers or clients, suppliers, the local community and government.

Organisations may communicate with customers and clients via their website, by **personalised email**, **phone** or **social media**. These methods are known as **communication platforms**.

Communication with team members in distant locations may include conference calls over the Internet using a webcam. A regular conference call can keep all team members up-to-date while saving time and the expense of all participants having to travel to a Head Office.

Selection of communication channels

While telephone calls, messages, chats and emails may be just right for communications between individuals and teams, sometimes an organisation needs to communicate with as many customers or potential new customers as possible.

Public status updates

A website is a vital communication platform for sharing data and information with stakeholders and for getting feedback.

- **Public status updates** may be displayed on a web page to give information about the status of new projects, services and products. A feature to enable reactions from readers may be included so that people can give their reactions and add comments.

- This enables an organisation to collect feedback from customers from any location at any time.

- Responses can be given either by sending a private message or shared on the website.

- Customer feedback can be analysed and used to improve a product or service, or provide more information about it where this is needed.

Using social media to communicate with stakeholders

Retailers and other organisations use social media for several reasons:

- To share news about new or improved products and services. This may be in the form of a **public status update**

- To post photographs of customers enjoying their products or facilities, or to encourage others to buy or join

- To get customer feedback on their products

- To learn what customers are saying about them so they can address any problems or offer new or improved services and products

- To manage and deal with complaints in a timely way

- To increase website traffic. Sharing content from your website to social media channels encourages visitors to visit the website

Social media is a very effective way of advertising. According to surveys carried out in 2017-18, between 70% and 80% of shoppers make buying decisions based on social media. Rather than believe advertisements, buyers tend to believe what their peers say.

Organisations can pay for advertisements to be sent to selected populations. Facebook, for example, will (for a fee per customer) target subscribers who fulfil categories specified by the sending organisation.

 Q2 **Explain the reasons why you use social media. Do you receive communications from people you don't know? If so, are these communications interesting, useful, offensive, welcome or unwelcome? Should there be more control over what is posted on social media sites?**

Personalised emails

It is relatively easy for an organisation using a mass mailing service to send a personalised email to all their existing customers to keep them informed of the latest products or latest news. In its simplest form, this is done by inserting a field name such as 'firstname' into the greeting, for example "Dear [`firstname`],". The different first names will be populated from a customer database.

Exercises

1. Davis & Gordon is a firm of architects. They have 30 employees.

   They have recently changed from a traditional server-based network to a cloud computing and cloud storage system.

   (a) Their cloud computing software makes it possible for them to create teams of architects and designers working from home as well as in the office.

   Explain **two** benefits to Davis and Gordon of allowing employees to work from home. [4]

   (b) Describe **three** tools available using cloud software that will make it easy for members of a team, some of them in the office and some working from home, to collaborate on a project. [6]

2. VillaHolidays is a travel company which organises week-long holidays for families and groups wanting to stay in a villa in Italy or Greece. Their head office is in London and they have a local manager in each area where they manage villas rented out by the owners.

   (a) Describe **two** modern technologies which help keep local managers informed about details of holiday bookings made by the head office in London. [4]

   (b) Holiday bookings can be made over the phone or online using the company website.

   Describe **two** reasons why customers may prefer to use the online booking system rather than the telephone. [4]

   (c) The company produces an online catalogue with one page for each villa that can be rented.

   They also publish a glossy, 400-page catalogue which they mail to all past customers and to anyone who requests a printed catalogue.

   Discuss the advantages and disadvantages of producing a printed catalogue in addition to having a website. [6]

Chapter 5
Inclusivity and accessibility

Objectives

- Describe how modern technologies aid inclusivity and accessibility:
  - interface design, accessibility features, flexibility of work hours and locations
- Describe positive and negative impacts of modern technology on organisations in terms of:
  - inclusivity, accessibility, remote working

Designing inclusive interfaces

There is a temptation for interface designers to design for people similar to themselves in terms of their:

- capabilities
- experience
- education
- expectation
- attitudes

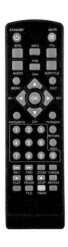

Perhaps this is why elderly people often have so much trouble in mastering the features of a mobile phone or a TV control. An interface designer needs to ask:

- What is the intended user group?
- Is the interface usable and accessible by as many people as possible?
- Is it aesthetically pleasing?

Note: More on the topic of providing equal access to all can be found in Chapter 14.

Q1 Describe how the user interface in an in-car satellite navigation system can be made accessible to all drivers, including those who cannot read or write.

Interface suitable for people with limited hand movement

Some people cannot easily control a mouse. One way of making it easier is to increase the size of the icons or buttons that they need to click on. Another way, in MS Windows, is to enable Sticky Keys so that instead of pressing two keys simultaneously, such as **Ctrl-S** for **Save**, the function can be activated by pressing the **Shift** key five times.

The mouse can also be controlled using the numeric keypad.

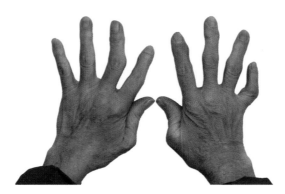

There are numerous settings in Windows to make software as accessible as possible.

If you are using Windows, search for "Accessibility settings". Click on each menu item in turn to view the options.

Interface settings for colour blind or partially sighted users

There are also settings for people with visual impairments. Reading online documents which rely on colour to impart a particular message, for example, red text for "This is important", may be difficult for some viewers. Colour-coded buttons for navigation on a website could also cause unnecessary problems. Adding text to a button is a simple method of ensuring that the navigation scheme is accessible to as many people as possible. Font sizes can be adjusted on most smartphone and PC operating systems.

Colour filters can be set in Windows for people with different types of colour blindness. A filter can be selected to make the nine colours on the wheel more distinct.

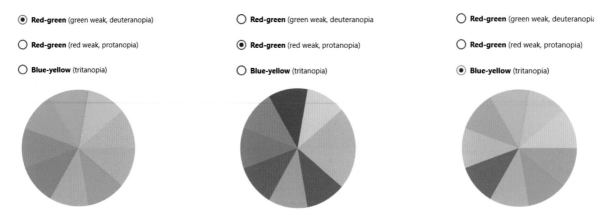

Layout and font

Windows also offers special options for partially sighted or blind users.

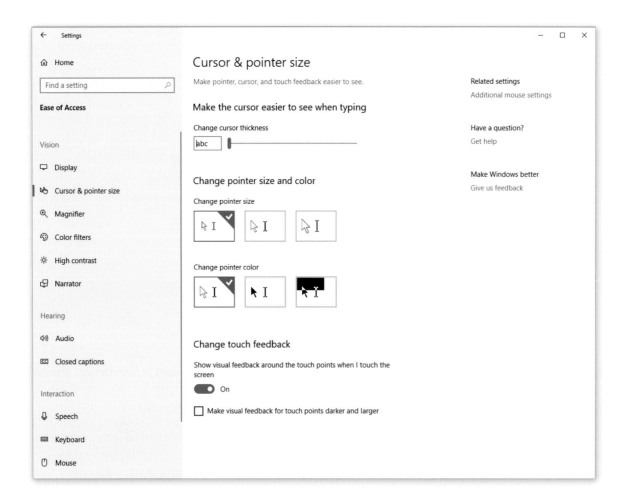

Making websites accessible

Designing for blind or partially sighted users

Web designers have a legal obligation to ensure that the websites they design can be accessed by blind and partially sighted people. With the help of **screen readers**, **synthesized text-to-speech** and **Braille display technology**, blind people can use the Web.

Some measures that can be implemented are:

- Provide **text labels** (Alt text) to describe images, and alternative content for all other media.
- Design for device independence. So a mouse is not required.
- Use simple language on the website, and specify the language used.

Designing for physically impaired users

- Provide buttons rather than text for navigation to provide a larger "target" for links.
- Use clear consistent layout and navigation.
- Be aware that not everyone uses a mouse.

 Q2 Find out the number of people in the UK who are registered blind or partially sighted. Why is it important for online retailers to make their websites accessible to this section of society?

Designing for deaf users

The use of closed captioning or subtitling moving images can make a website more inclusive for deaf people. Description tags can also be added to web page elements that may help to describe any audible signals normally present.

Flexibility of work hours and locations

Modern technology has made it possible for many IT employees and freelancers to work from home or another location, and not have to travel to the office every day. This can aid inclusivity.

- **Free software for transferring large files** is readily available and easy to use.
- **Cloud storage** means that data is accessible from any location with an Internet connection.
- **Cloud computing** means that software can be accessed from any location with an Internet connection. Working from home, a consultant, designer, social media expert, marketing manager and hundreds of other employees working in different jobs can load the software that they need from the cloud. The files that they save in the cloud will be accessible to any authorised person, wherever they are, and at any time of day.
- **Fast broadband connections** enable software and data to be downloaded from the cloud in no more time than it takes to load from a hard disk.

Note: Advantages and disadvantages of remote working are covered in Chapter 6.

Exercises

1. Susan is a partially sighted programmer working in the head office of a large software company.

   (a) Describe three ways in which the operating system interface can be adjusted for Susan to make it easier for her to use it effectively. [6]

   (b) Susan is married with two small children.

   Discuss the advantages and disadvantages to Susan of an arrangement whereby she can work at home for three days of the week. [6]

2. Websites can be made more accessible for people with disabilities.

   (a) Describe **two** features of a website which can help to make it accessible to a deaf person. [4]

   (b) Describe **two** benefits to a company of making a website accessible to people with disabilities. [4]

Chapter 6
Impacts of modern technologies

Objectives

- Describe positive and negative impacts of modern technologies on organisations in terms of:
  - required infrastructure, demand on infrastructure of chosen tools/platforms, availability of infrastructure, 24/7 access, security of distributed/dispersed data, collaboration, inclusivity, accessibility, remote working

- Describe positive and negative impacts of modern technologies on individuals:
  - flexibility (home/remote working), working styles (choice of time, device, location), impact on individual mental wellbeing

Impacts of modern technologies on organisations

Infrastructure

Required infrastructure: No modern organisation of any size can operate without the use of technology. However, a significant number of small businesses do not have their own websites. Less than 10% of businesses with fewer than 10 employees make **e-commerce sales**.

Demand on infrastructure: Among those who do make e-commerce sales, many are not making the most of their online sales ability because their websites are not optimised for use on smartphones. In 2017, it was predicted that shoppers would double the amount they spent on purchases made on mobile devices the following year.

Availability of infrastructure: A fast broadband Internet connection is essential for a business that uses cloud computing or storage. In 2017, 62% of businesses with 1,000 or more employees had superfast broadband, but less than 6% of businesses with fewer than 10 employees had this Internet speed.

Cloud storage: Cloud storage has enabled organisations to operate effectively without having to buy expensive, high-capacity file servers for their networks. Instead, using a cloud storage provider they can pay for the amount of data storage that they need.

Cloud storage gives organisations the following benefits:

- It is scalable; when an organisation's storage needs increase, they can pay for more storage. Without cloud storage they would have the expense and disruption of buying a new, larger-capacity file server. They might decide to allow for future expansion, so that much of the capacity might be unused for several years.

- Data held in the cloud is automatically backed up, with older versions of files that have since been updated available for several months.

- The data is accessible from anywhere in the world with an Internet connection.

- Recovery from a disaster such as a fire or flood will be much easier as their data will be unaffected.

Cloud computing enables team collaboration, automatic updates and software maintenance.

However, without a fast broadband connection, slow upload and download speeds will have a negative effect on productivity.

Larger companies, with more cash and expertise at their disposal, are better able to make full use of the latest communication technologies, devices and web-based platforms.

Security

Keeping data secure is a major concern for all organisations handling personal data.

Data protection used to mean having good backup procedures so that data was not accidentally lost or destroyed. This is still important, but there are other factors as well.

- Backup copies must be properly managed, available, reliable and secure. Data must be available when it is most needed.

- Network data is vulnerable when employees are able to download data to their mobile devices, which could be lost or stolen.

- Cloud storage is not 100% secure. Increased cyber-terrorism is a very effective way of creating chaos; damaging large banking systems, water or electrical supply systems could have devastating impacts.

Dispersed and distributed data

Data may be broken up into smaller data sets, which are then stored along with coded information about some of the other data subsets, on different storage devices, often in different geographical locations. The original data can then be recreated from these data subsets.

Collaboration

Cloud technology, available 24/7 and around the globe, has enabled people to collaborate on projects, wherever they are located. Video calls made over the Internet mean that a group of people can participate in team meetings. Software such as Microsoft Teams combines workplace chat, meetings, notes and attachments. Shared calendars and project management software helps keep everyone on track and in the know.

A group of people having an evening video conference meeting with someone in another time zone

Flexibility of working hours, styles and locations

Modern communications and cloud technologies make it possible for employees to work from home, even in another country. Hours can also be flexible, and where necessary cater for different time zones.

There are many advantages both for the employer and the employee. For the employer:

- They can recruit from a much larger pool of talent.
- They do not have to provide office space including desk space, increased toilet and leisure space, car parking or other facilities.
- Employees working from home are often hard-working and loyal, appreciating the freedom that flexible working gives them.
- Security during data transmission.

Modern technology allows data to be kept **secure** while it is being transmitted to and from different locations. Using a **virtual private network (VPN)**, all data transmitted to or from a computer logged in to the network from any location, to the main head office, is automatically encrypted so that it even if it is hacked by a cybercriminal, it cannot be read. This enables employees staying in a hotel while travelling, for example, to use an open Wi-Fi network provided by the hotel and still be able to safely log in to the office network via the Internet over a secure connection.

In 2018, a survey found that 97% of organisations were using cloud technology. This percentage has been increasing year on year from a tiny percentage in 2008. On average, in 2018 these organisations used approximately five different clouds.

Explain the reasons for this rapid growth in cloud computing and cloud storage.

Inclusivity and accessibility

Organisations have legal obligations to ensure that everyone has equal opportunities in education and employment. Technology can assist greatly, and employers and software designers must make special provisions for people with a disability.

Some of the ways of making technology accessible and inclusive are covered in Chapter 5.

Impacts of modern technologies on individuals

Flexibility of working hours, styles and locations

Advantages for employees working from home include:

- They do not have to spend time in commuting, sitting in traffic jams or standing on crowded, delayed trains.
- They save the expense of commuting.
- They may be able to live more cheaply in the countryside rather than close to the office.
- Hours are flexible; some people prefer to work early in the mornings or late at night.
- Children's needs can be fitted around work hours more easily.
- People with a disability may find it easier to work at home in their own environment with their own specialised hardware and software.

On the other hand, some employees may miss the buzz of a busy office, and may feel excluded from casual social events. They may find it is lonely and depressing working on their own all day. They may also miss the same opportunities to make friends.

Impact on individual mental well-being

In addition to the impact of digital technologies on opportunities from individuals to work from home, social media and gaming have had an enormous impact, both positive and negative, on the mental well-being of many individuals. Whilst typically affecting teenagers and young adults, older people and others may also feel isolated by reasons of disability or other circumstances.

- Social media and text messaging have become an integral part of how individuals communicate with their social groups. According to statistics, British adults check their mobile phones on average every 12 minutes, and about 40% of adults check their phone within about 5 minutes of waking up.

- Constant checking can have an effect on physical and mental health. Constant checkers can feel disconnected from their family, even when they are in the same room.

- Too much time spent on social media is associated with an increased risk of loneliness and depression.

- Users of social media might experience increased levels of social dissatisfaction and unhappiness as a result of comparing their happiness and popularity to that of their friends.

- Harmful social media sites encouraging young people to starve themselves or even commit suicide can have devastating effects.

- Well-known people or activists (especially women) are frequently trolled on social media, receiving harassment and threats of rape and murder for their opinions. Caroline Criado-Perez, who successfully campaigned for a woman to be represented on a banknote, and for a statue of Millicent Fawcett, a female suffragist in the early 20th century, to be erected in Parliament Square, reported that at one point she was receiving about 50 such threats every hour. At the height of the abuse, Craido-Perez "lost half a stone in two days" and "couldn't eat or sleep". She commented later: "I don't know if I had a kind of breakdown. I was unable to function, unable to have normal interactions."

In April 2019, the government published a long-awaited white paper to announce their intention of introducing legislation to force Internet companies "to take reasonable steps to keep their users safe and tackle illegal and harmful activity on their services."

Q2 **Describe some of the ways in which you use modern technology outside the classroom. Do you think modern technology has had a positive impact on most people's lives? Has it had a negative impact on some people?**

Exercises

1. Thomas owns a gym. Members book sessions on his website.

   Thomas uses cloud software for gym management and to plan his staff rota. Gym coaches log into the planning software to enter the hours that they are available to take classes or individual coaching sessions the following week. All the data on coaches and gym members is held in cloud storage.

   (a) Describe **two** benefits of using a cloud provider in regard to the security of data. [4]

   (b) Describe **two** essential elements of infrastructure that are required for the gym's IT systems. [4]

   (c) Describe **one** drawback of using cloud software. [2]

2. Children are increasingly using many modern-day technologies including smartphones, social media, file sharing, and streaming services at a younger and younger age.

   (a) Explain **two** ways in which younger users can suffer from the use of such technologies. [4]

   (b) Discuss the positive impacts on teenagers of using modern day technology. [6]

Cyber security

In this section:

Chapter 7
System attacks and external threats

Objectives

- Understand the reasons why systems are attacked
- Understand the terms hacking and 'black hat'
- Describe the following external threats to systems and data:
    - Unauthorised access
    - Malware (virus, worms, botnet, rootkit, Trojan, ransomware, spyware)
    - Denial of Service (DoS) attacks
    - Phishing, pharming, social engineering, shoulder surfing
    - 'Man-in-the-middle' attacks

Threats to digital systems and data

News stories featuring hacking attacks on high profile organisations and data breaches affecting thousands of people appear almost every day in the media.

An **organisation** is a group of people who work together in a structured way for a shared purpose. Companies, businesses, schools, charities, hospitals and government departments are all types of organisations.

All organisations have digital systems and data that are critical to their daily operations. If their computers stop working, the performance of their network deteriorates, or sensitive data is stolen, the consequences will be serious.

A **threat** is an incident or an action – deliberate or unintended – that results in disruption, down-time or data loss. Threats include natural disasters, such as a fire or a flood, technical failures such as a power outage or a malfunctioning server, as well as accidental or malicious actions carried out by people. An internal threat is caused by an event or activity that occurs inside an organisation. External threats originate on the outside.

An **attack** is a deliberate action, targeting an organisation's digital systems or data, carried out by a person or group of people with malicious intent. Attackers may be people on the outside who exploit security vulnerabilities to break into an organisation's digital systems. Or they may be 'insiders' – people working for an organisation who have access to its systems.

Case study:
Hacker attack on British Airways

Between 21 August and 5 September 2018, hackers launched a major attack on British Airways, stealing email addresses and credit card details belonging to 380,000 of the airline's customers. Not only did the breach cost the company a lot of money, it also severely damaged its reputation. Some previously loyal customers said they no longer trusted British Airways and vowed never to fly with them again.

Why systems are attacked

Some people carry out an attack simply for **fun**. They enjoy the **challenge** of breaching the security defences an organisation has in place and like to show off their abilities, often boasting of the success of their attacks on social media.

Financial gain is a powerful incentive. Serious amounts of money can be made from selling stolen data or using stolen information to perpetrate fraud.

Some companies pay attackers to carry out **industrial espionage** on their behalf, spying on competitors, stealing intellectual property and trade secrets or sabotaging their activities. State-sponsored espionage is also increasingly common.

Someone who feels victimised, badly done by, or bears a grudge may launch a **personal attack** on an organisation.

So-called '**hacktivists**' attack digital systems to make a political statement or show their disapproval.

Back in 1989, hacktivists released malware called 'Worms Against Nuclear Killers' into NASA's network in protest against the launch of the nuclear-powered rocket carrying the Galileo probe into orbit. The attack is thought to have cost half a million dollars in lost time and resources

Q1 Why might the Driving and Vehicle Licencing Agency (DVLA) be attacked?

Why might a pharmaceutical company be attacked?

External threats to digital systems and data security

Unauthorised access

Unauthorised access refers to someone gaining entry without permission to an organisation's network, computers, software or data. This is achieved by exploiting a **security vulnerability** – an unintended flaw in a system or piece of software, such as an operating system.

A **hacker** is someone who seeks out and exploits security vulnerabilities, in order to gain unauthorised access to digital systems and the data they hold. When the motive for hacking is criminal, the perpetrator is often referred to as a **black hat hacker**.

Around one third of UK businesses experienced some form of hacking attack during the course of 2018, with some being attacked several times a day. In the UK, as in most other countries, hacking is a criminal offence. The Computer Misuse Act is used to prosecute hackers. You can find out more about this legislation In Chapter 17.

Malware

The term malware is a derived from the words '**mal**icious' and 'soft**ware**'. Malware is an umbrella term for malicious software that is designed to harm a digital system, damage data or harvest sensitive information. There are millions of malware programs in existence already and new ones are being written and released every day.

Two of the most common types of malware are viruses and worms. Both are highly contagious, spreading 'infection' from one computer to another by making copies of themselves – a process known as **self-replication**.

A **virus** is a piece of malicious code that attaches to a legitimate program . When a user runs the 'host' program, the virus is activated. Viruses spread by making copies of themselves and inserting them into other programs.

Actions such as opening an infected email attachment or visiting a malicious website spread a viral infection. Computer viruses are almost always harmful, causing damage to hardware, software and data.

A **worm** is similar to a virus, but – unlike a virus – it is a self-contained program, capable of spreading on its own, without help from humans and without having to attach itself to another program. Worms get around by exploiting vulnerabilities in network operating systems or by attaching themselves to emails. They self-replicate at a tremendous rate, using up hard drive space and bandwidth, overloading servers and affecting network performance. A badly infected network will eventually stop working altogether.

Case study: The ILOVEYOU worm

Originating in the Philippines in May 2000, the ILOVEYOU worm spread to more than 50 million computers worldwide in just ten days. It infiltrated victims' address books, sending copies of itself to all their contacts.

Named after the wooden horse used by the ancient Greeks to infiltrate the city of Troy, a Trojan is hidden inside legitimate software, which users are tricked into downloading. Once installed on a computer, a Trojan works undercover to carry out a pre-determined task, such as creating a backdoor for hackers to use, installing other harmful programs or harvesting sensitive data and transmitting it to someone on the outside.

Case study: The Zeus Trojan

In the summer of 2010, the Zeus Trojan was used to steal money from over 3000 UK bank accounts. Posing as a security app, the Trojan harvested personal data, including account numbers and login details, that enabled hackers to transfer large sums of money to themselves from victims' accounts.

 Viruses, worms and Trojans are all types of malware. How does each of them work? What damage can they do to an organisation?

A **rootkit** is a set of tools that give a hacker high-level administrative control of a computer. They can then use this privileged position to encrypt files, install programs, change system configurations or steal data. Like Trojans, rootkits often come bundled with legitimate software that a user chooses to download. They can also be installed on unattended computers when no-one is looking.

Some malware is designed to enable criminals to extort or steal money from organisations. **Ransomware** encrypts files stored on a computer system, making them unreadable. Victims must pay a ransom – usually in Bitcoins that are impossible to trace – to get the files unlocked. A deadline is usually set for payment of the ransom. If the payment isn't received by then, the amount demanded increases or the files are permanently locked. Ransomware is spread via email attachments or through infected websites. Trojans are often implicated in ransomware attacks.

Case study: Ransomware attack on the NHS

In 2017, the WannaCry ransomware attacked computers running outdated MS Windows software. The hackers responsible demanded a ransom payment to unlock the files on each infected computer. NHS computer systems were targeted, forcing thousands of appointments and operations to be cancelled. The NHS refused to pay the ransom, but many victims – anxious to regain access to their data – did so. No-one knows for certain how much money the hackers netted.

Criminals use **spyware** to harvest personal information, such as passwords, credit card numbers and email addresses from computers. Armed with this information, they can steal a user's identity, siphon off money from their bank account or make purchases using their credit card. Emails, instant messages and social media are all potential sources of spyware. Once installed on a computer, spyware works in the background without being noticed, periodically sending out the data it has stolen to someone on the outside.

Case study: Spyware harvests personal data from mobile phones

RedDrop is an invasive form of mobile phone spyware, disguised as a set of useful tools such as image editors, calculators and language-learning apps, to persuade phone owners to download it.

Once installed on a phone, RedDrop harvests user data, photos, contacts and even recordings of nearby audio, whilst secretly sending text messages to a premium-rate phone number, racking up a massive bill.

The term **botnet** is derived from the words 'ro**bot**' and '**net**work'. A botnet is an army of 'zombie' devices. Botnets are used to carry out mass attacks, such as emailing spam out to millions of Internet users or shutting down a website by bombarding it with traffic.

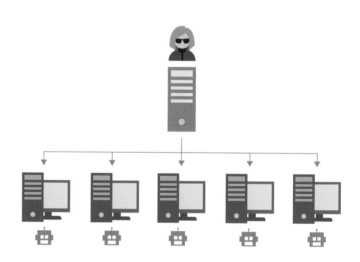

Computers are not the only devices that can be taken over to become part of a botnet. Any Internet of Things (IoT) device with poor security – smart TVs, fitness trackers, fridges and even medical implants – can be 'zombified'. In just two weeks over Christmas 2013, a botnet, made up of more than 100,000 devices, sent out 750,000 spam and phishing messages.

Crypto-mining is becoming an increasingly common use for botnets. Criminals use the combined processing power of their zombie army to 'mine' for cryptocurrency such as Bitcoins.

In a **denial of service attack**, one or more computers or other types of digital device are used to bring down a website by flooding it with a huge volume of traffic, such as repeated login requests. The objective of the attack is to cause disruption and inconvenience rather than long term damage.

Case study: Denial-of-service attack knocks out the National Lottery

On September 30th, 2017, a denial of service attack knocked out the National Lottery's website for about 90 minutes just before the draw was about to take place. People were prevented from playing the lottery online, potentially missing out on the chance to win millions of pounds. The perpetrators of the attack remain unknown as does their motive.

Q3 **Botnets are often used to carry out denial of service attacks. Why do you think this is?**

Social engineering: phishing, blagging and shoulder-surfing

It is far easier and quicker to con people into revealing information than it is to create and deploy spyware to steal it.

Social engineering involves tricking people into divulging valuable information about themselves – passwords, PINs, credit card numbers, bank account details. It works by playing on human emotions, such as curiosity, fear, or greed.

The ILOVEYOU computer worm tricked people into spreading it by piquing their curiosity. Victims received an email with an attached 'love letter'. When they opened the attachment, the worm copied itself to all the contacts in their address book.

The term '**phishing**' comes from 'fishing'. A 'phisherman' dangles a 'baited hook' in the hope that at least some of the fish in the pool will swallow it. Targets of a phishing attack receive an email, a text message (SMiShing) or a phone call (vishing) from what appears to be a trustworthy source – their Internet service provider, their bank, someone at work. Believing that the communication is genuine, they do what is asked of them – downloading an attachment or clicking on a link.

This email contains what appears to be a very attractive offer.

Hamish Davidson <info@db.online.

A database with the potential to change your business

To: David Jones djones@smartthings.co.uk

Reply-To: info@db.online

WE HAVE DECIDED TO GIVE AWAY OUR NEW BUSINESS DATABASE TO YOU.

Dear manager,

Over the last few years, our databases have helped hundreds of British businesses like yours find new customers and achieve growth.

Today I am delighted to announce the release of our latest database, DBEXEC 19.

DBExec 19 gives you access to 30,000 senior executives from the largest 5000 companies in the UK including their direct email addresses (no info@ or contact@ emails) and best phone numbers to reach them.

Whether you want direct access to the CEO's from the largest supermarkets, the largest banks or the UK's largest companies, our new database has the potential to transform your business.

And best of all is that you get unlimited acess to the whole data.

We have decided to give away our new database for only £29 instead of £1498 (98% off) to the **first 100 customers placing their order today before 3PM.**

To find out more about our new database or download a free sample click here.

If you are happy with it, place your order today before 3PM to profit from your substantial discount.

To your success,

Best Regards,

Hamish Davidson
Head of Marketing

Unsubscribe:
Click here if you do not want to receive any more emails from us.

 Q4   What are the tell-tale signs that this is a phishing email?

Sometimes, rather than casting out bait indiscriminately to lots of people, a specific person is targeted – a tactic known as **spear phishing**. The target of a spear phishing attack is usually somebody who holds a senior position within an organisation, with access to highly valuable sensitive information. The attacker typically spends a considerable amount of time finding out as much as they can about the intended target in order to gain their trust.

Blagging is another form of social engineering. The 'blagger' invents a scenario to persuade their victim to divulge sensitive information. They might, for example, pretend to be a member of the IT department phoning to inform a user that malware has been detected on their laptop, requiring up-dated anti-virus protection to be installed immediately. By stressing the urgency of the situation, the 'blagger' puts pressure on the user to hand over their ID and password.

In some cases, attackers use less sophisticated methods of social engineering to get what they want.

Shoulder surfing involves acquiring sensitive information, such as passwords and PINs by direct observation. Sometimes it really does involve someone peering over a user's shoulder when they are using their laptop or tablet. But shoulder surfing can also take place at a distance, using binoculars, video cameras, drones or vision-enhancing devices.

Pharming and man-in-the middle attacks

Not all successful attacks rely on social engineering tactics to gain information from victims. Some, like pharming and man-in-the-middle attacks use technical knowhow instead.

Pharming involves redirecting people to a bogus, look-a-like website without them realising what has happened. One way of achieving this is to change the IP address of a website stored locally in a computer's DNS cache. However, many more people can be caught out if attackers are able to hack into an ISP's DNS server and modify an address stored there.

The objective of a pharming attack is to acquire sensitive personal information or to install malware on a victim's computer.

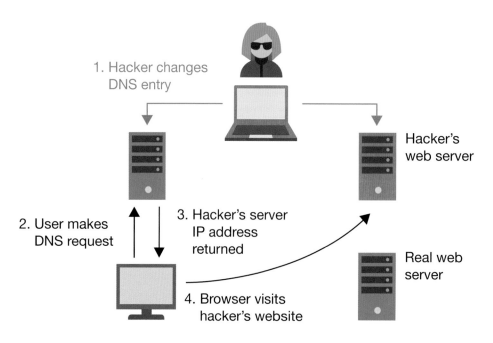

1. Hacker changes DNS entry
2. User makes DNS request
3. Hacker's server IP address returned
4. Browser visits hacker's website

Hacker's web server

Real web server

Case study: Pharming attack affects 50 financial institutions

In February 2017, 50 financial institutions, including Barclays Bank, the Bank of Scotland, PayPal, eBay and American Express, were targeted in a sophisticated pharming attack. Attackers constructed a look-alike website for each company. A Trojan was used to deliver malware to customers' computers. When customers subsequently typed in the URL of one of the affected companies, they were first redirected to a look-alike website that captured their account login information, before being redirected to the real site. Customers remained unaware of what was happening throughout.

A **man-in-the-middle attack** is one in which communications between two parties – the sender and recipient – are intercepted by a third – the so-called 'man in the middle'. Neither the sender or the recipient are aware of the presence of an eavesdropper. Emails, text messages or social media posts for example, can all be viewed by the man in the middle. One popular way of orchestrating a man-in-the-middle attack is to set up a fake Wi-Fi hotspot in a public area. All the man in the middle has to do then is sit back and wait for people to connect to it.

Exercises

1. A malware attack can have serious consequences for an organisation.

   Describe **two** types of disruption a malware attack can cause. [4]

2. SmartThings is a UK-based company that develops Internet of Things (IoT) solutions for the home. Since its set up in 2012, the company has been targeted several times by hackers.

   (a) Explain what is meant by the term 'hacking'. [2]

   (b) Give **four** reasons why a hacker might attack the company's digital systems. [4]

   (c) The company found and repaired vulnerabilities that could lead to a ransomware attack.

   Describe how a ransomware attack works. [3]

3. Social engineering works by manipulating people into voluntarily giving away information.

   Describe **two** techniques used in social engineering attacks. [4]

4. ActivWear is an online clothing company which sends out printed catalogues to thousands of customers on its mailing list. It accepts orders online, by mail or by telephone.

   Discuss the external threats, both deliberate and accidental, to ActivWear's computer systems which may have serious consequences for the organisation. [6]

Chapter 8
Internal threats and impact of breaches

Objectives

- Understand internal threats to digital systems and data security:
  - unintentional disclosure of data
  - visiting untrustworthy websites and downloading files from the Internet
  - use of portable storage devices
  - users overriding security controls
  - intentional stealing or leaking of information

- Understand the impact of security breaches on organisations:
  - data and financial loss
  - damage to public image
  - reduction in productivity and downtime
  - legal action

Internal threats to digital systems and data security

External hacking attacks may be the ones that hit the headlines, but, in reality, insiders pose a much bigger security risk to an organisation's digital systems and data.

Insiders are trusted individuals – employees, contractors, suppliers, students on work experience – who have permission to access an organisation's buildings, equipment and files. Not surprisingly, it is much more difficult for an organisation to defend itself against insider threats than it is to defend against external attacks.

Unintentional disclosure of data

Not all insider threats are malicious. Around 75% are down to human error. Carelessness, failure to follow policies and procedures and being ignorant of the risks are the biggest problems.

An insider can unintentionally disclose data by:

Being careless, e.g.

- accidentally deleting an important file
- losing a laptop or USB flash drive
- sending an email to the wrong person or to everyone in a distribution list rather than just the intended recipient

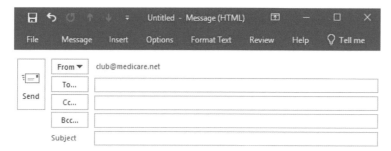

Failing to follow policies and procedures, e.g.

- leaving an office computer unattended and unlocked
- choosing a weak password, writing it down somewhere or failing to change it regularly
- assisting someone without proper authentication to gain entry to a restricted area, e.g. by lending them an ID card or divulging the access code
- throwing sensitive information into the rubbish bin where a so-called 'dumpster diver', an office cleaner, someone servicing the photocopier or watering the office plants – might find it
- transferring confidential company data to an insecure home network

Not understanding the risks, such as:

- visiting an untrustworthy website and downloading files from the Internet
- opening emails and attachments from unknown sources
- failing to recognise the tell-tale signs of a phishing email
- not realising that a USB flash drive found lying around may contain harmful malware

Visiting untrustworthy websites and downloading files from the Internet

Untrustworthy websites are malicious sites that look harmless, so that visitors are fooled into giving away sensitive information or downloading malware.

Even trustworthy websites are not always what they seem. Malicious code can be inserted into advertisements that appear on popular websites. When a visitor clicks on an infected advert, malware is downloaded onto their computer.

A so-called **drive-by download** occurs when malware downloads and installs itself onto a computer without the user doing anything more than simply landing on a drive-by-download site.

Search engine poisoning is one tactic used to drive unsuspecting visitors to untrustworthy websites. The sites are packed with trending keywords so that they appear high up in a search engine's rankings, making it likely that people will select them.

If an employee downloads music, videos, or software from a **peer-to-peer file sharing site** onto their work computer, they may well get more than they bargained for. Harmful malware may be bundled along with files downloaded from these sites.

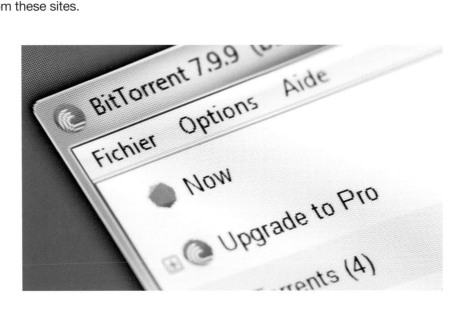

The consequences of employees visiting untrustworthy websites or downloading files from the Internet can be very serious.

- Downloaded malware can quickly spread across the whole network causing damage and disruption.
- Armed with a valid user ID and password, a hacker can steal sensitive data, launch a ransomware attack or sabotage operations.
- If an employee downloads copyrighted material, such as music tracks or videos, onto their work computer, the organisation could be legally liable for it.
- Watching video such as football matches or listening to music online consumes bandwidth. The performance of the network will suffer, affecting everyone else trying to work.
- Employees wasting time on non-work-related Internet activities costs the company money as they are less productive.

Use of portable storage devices

Nowadays many employees work from home or on the move. Portable storage devices, such as USB flash drives, are useful for carrying around large amounts of data. The downside is that they are easily lost or stolen, increasing the risk to any sensitive data stored on them.

Hackers have been known to load USB flash drives with malware and leave them in an office car park in the hope that unsuspecting employees will pick them up. The drives are set to run automatically when inserted into a computer, installing key logger malware to harvest usernames and passwords.

USB flash drives are also a convenient means of removing stolen data from an organisation without anyone noticing.

Users overriding security controls

Security controls are designed to reduce the risk to an organisation's digital systems and data. Physical controls limit access to buildings, rooms and equipment. Logical controls limit access to software, data and the Internet.

Unfortunately, the drawback of having effective security controls is that they make systems less convenient to use and everyday tasks more time-consuming to complete. This prompts some employees to find ways to side-step them.

- If passwords have to be long and complex, people will be tempted to write them down.
- Wedging open a door that is meant to be kept locked may save time when moving between buildings, but runs the risk of providing an intruder with an easy way in.
- Throwing confidential material into a desk bin may be quicker than getting up and taking it to the shredder, but risks it being found by an unscrupulous co-worker who spots a chance to make money from it.
- Lending a security badge to a visitor so that they can go to the toilet may be a kind thing to do, but also gives them unsupervised access to parts of the building that are out of bounds.

Intentional stealing or leaking of information

Malicious insiders don't need to install malware or exploit a vulnerability in order to carry out an attack.

- If insiders have genuine network logins, they can access files stored on the network.
- They may overhear confidential conversations taking place in the corridor or find sensitive information left in rubbish bins or on display boards for example.
- They are well placed to take advantage of unlocked computers and guessable passwords.

Case study: Insider attacks on Apple

In a memo sent to all its employees in April 2018, Apple disclosed that 29 insiders had been caught leaking confidential information about future plans to the media during the previous 12 months. They all lost their jobs and some were charged with criminal offences.

The memo went on to explain how leaked information about a new product can negatively impact sales of current models, give rivals more time to begin developing a competitive product in response, and can lead to fewer sales when the new product launches.

Sometimes insiders are targeted by outsiders – members of the press, people working for competitors – who befriend them on professional and social networks like LinkedIn and Facebook and use flattery to pry for information. Or they may be whistle blowers, keen to draw attention to something their employer is doing that they believe is wrong.

Case study: Classified US army information passed to WikiLeaks

While deployed in Iraq, Private Bradley Manning downloaded more than 500,000 US army reports and classified combat videos and passed them on to WikiLeaks.

 Q1 **Why is it difficult for organisations to defend themselves against internal attacks?**

Impact of a security breach

A **security breach** is an incident in which an organisation's security defences are bypassed, enabling someone to gain unauthorised access to confidential data such as IDs and passwords, email addresses, customer lists, software source code, sensitive financial information or intellectual property. Security breaches impact on organisations in a variety of ways – all of them damaging.

 Q2 **List five ways in which an organisation's security defences can be bypassed.**

Data and financial loss

A security breach – whether originating inside or outside an organisation – is likely to result in substantial financial loss.

- If an organisation's systems are down, customers are likely to go elsewhere for the products and services they want and may not return.

- Time-critical activities may not be completed on time, resulting in financial penalties and lost business.

- Salaries still have to be paid, even though employees are unable to carry out their work.

If, as a result of a security breach, a company's **intellectual property** (product designs, trade secrets, formulas or customer lists, etc.) falls into the hands of a rival, its competitiveness will be damaged, its share of the market will decline and its revenue will drop.

Extra costs are also likely to be incurred as a result of a security breach.

- IT staff may have to work overtime or be diverted from other tasks in order to investigate and deal with the breach. Additional temporary staff may need to be hired.

- Damaged computers will have to be repaired or replaced.

- Any lost data must be recreated or restored from backups.

- Hackers may extort money by encrypting files or threatening to reveal sensitive information.

- A call centre may need to be set up to inform customers and answer their queries.

- Legal costs may be incurred, and compensation claims may have to be paid.

Damage to public image

An organisation's reputation is one of its greatest assets. It takes a long time to build, but just one high profile security breach is enough to cause serious harm. Owing to social media, bad news travels fast. A data breach in the UK will affect public perception of an organisation worldwide, impacting on its relationships with key stakeholders – customers, suppliers, shareholders, etc.

Case study: Two major data breaches damage trust in Facebook

Early in 2018 it emerged that data from around 87 million Facebook user accounts had been harvested illegally by Cambridge Analytica to build an algorithm that delivered targeted political adverts. The algorithm is believed to have influenced the outcomes of the 2016 US presidential election campaign and the UK EU referendum.

Later that year, Facebook suffered a second major security breach in which data from around 50 million of its users was compromised.

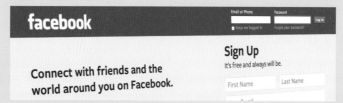

In a survey to assess how badly the company's reputation had been damaged, 40% of respondents said they did not trust Facebook to keep their personal information safe and intended to stop using it.

Among the steps Facebook subsequently took to rebuild public confidence was a television campaign in which it promised to do more to keep users safe and protect their privacy.

Rebuilding trust and repairing reputational damage is likely to take many years. In some cases, an organisation's public image never fully recovers.

 Q3   **How can an organisation repair a damaged reputation?**

Reduction in productivity and downtime

A security breach usually results in a period of **downtime**, during which an organisation's network and computer systems are shut down and unavailable for use. They may remain down for several days, preventing staff from working normally. Some employees are likely to find this very stressful, especially if they have to respond to angry customers.

Additional security measures put in place to avoid a repetition of the breach could make it more time-consuming for employees to do their jobs and their productivity will suffer.

Legal action

A new, updated **Data Protection Act** came into force in the UK in 2018. It is designed to protect individuals against misuse of their personal data. It stipulates that organisations must keep people's data secure. If a data breach occurs, they must notify the Information Commissioner's Office (ICO) within 72 hours and pay compensation to all those affected. Should they fail to do so they will be fined heavily.

Facebook was fined £500,000 – the maximum amount possible – for its part in the Cambridge Analytica scandal. They may also face law suits brought by people claiming material and/or non-material damage as a consequence of the breach. You can find out more about the Data Protection Act in Chapter 16.

Q4   **What do you think would be the impact on an aircraft manufacturer if hackers were to demonstrate that they were able to hack into the on-board computer system of one of its planes?**

Exercises

1.   QDS is a global mining company. It employs over 3000 people in sites all over the world. The company's digital systems and data are vulnerable to external and internal threats.

   (a)   Explain **two** ways in which an internal attack differs from an external attack.   [4]

   (b)   QDS has put in place a number of security controls to protect its digital systems and data.

         Explain **two** reasons why employees may be tempted to override these security controls.   [4]

   (c)   Explain **two** ways in which employees' use of portable storage devices, such as flash memory
         drives, poses a security risk.   [4]

2.   Credit2000 is a credit card company which has more than one million customers. Shoppers use their cards to pay for goods at tills in stores, or when ordering goods or services online.

     Discuss the impact that unauthorised access to personal data stored on company computers could have on Credit2000.   [6]

Chapter 9
User restrictions and finding weaknesses

Objectives

- Understand measures used to protect digital systems and reduce the impact of threats
- Understand methods of restricting user access:
  - physical security measures (locks)
  - passwords
  - using correct settings and levels of permitted access
  - biometrics
  - two-factor authentication
- Understand methods of finding weaknesses and improving system security:
  - ethical hacking (white hat, grey hat)
  - penetration testing
  - system and behaviour analysis

User access restriction

A key way of protecting an organisation's digital systems and data is to limit who has access to them.

Physical security measures

Physical security measures are used to restrict access to buildings, rooms and equipment.

They include:

- perimeter fencing to prevent passers-by from entering the premises
- protective barriers to prevent forced entry by people or vehicles
- locked doors that can only be opened by people with a key or access control card
- locked and barred windows to prevent intruders from breaking in
- security guards to cover all entry points and patrol the building
- scanning equipment to screen people entering and leaving the building
- use of smart cards or biometric identification to ensure that only authorised people can access a restricted area
- surveillance cameras and sensors to monitor activity in and around the building
- burglar alarm system to raise the alarm if an intruder manages to gain access
- smoke and heat detectors and firefighting equipment to protect against fire
- RFID tags fitted to computer equipment to thwart attempts to remove them from the building
- security cables to physically lock down computer equipment

Access control and authentication

Different employees require different levels of access, depending on their job role. Someone working in the canteen, for example, doesn't need to get into the server room or view sales figures and growth forecasts, but they will need to be able to use the lift, use washroom facilities, operate a till and order in fresh supplies.

Access control systems are used to control who is allowed to go where, who can log in to the network and which equipment they can use.

Authentication is the process of verifying the identity of a person seeking access. Authentication methods include passwords, swipe cards, biometric scans and electronic keys.

Authentication and access control are usually combined into a single operation, so that access is permitted based on successful authentication.

Passwords

Passwords are the most basic form of authentication. It is estimated that the average person has nearly 200 passwords.

The person who creates a password is supposed to be the only one who knows what it is. But therein lies a problem!

- People have a tendency to select weak passwords – ones that are easy to remember and therefore easy to guess. Three of the most popular passwords in 2018 were '123456', 'password' and 'qwerty'.

- Instead of choosing a unique password for each account, people often use the same password for all of them, meaning that if one gets compromised they all do.

- Rather than memorise their passwords, people often write them down, sometimes leaving them in conspicuous places such as on a post-it note stuck to their screen.

- People who fall victim to some form of social engineering attack give their password away voluntarily.

- A hacker, using key-logger software or spyware, can steal a password while it is being entered by a user. They may then be able to gain unauthorised access to a database containing all employees' passwords.

If an attacker gets hold of an employee's password they could install malware on the network, damage, destroy or steal sensitive data.

For a password to be effective, it needs to be:

- **Easy to remember, but hard to guess.**
  The advice used to be that a password should be at least eight characters long and consist of a combination of alphanumeric characters and symbols. However, it has now been shown that compound phrases with easy-to-remember words are much harder to crack.

- **Changed regularly** and immediately after a security breach. Left to their own devices, most users will take the easy option and make only minor changes, minimising the benefit.

How secure is your password?

Tip: Stronger passwords use different types of characters

Show password: ☐

●●●●●●●●●●●●●● ↑˅

Very Strong

15 characters containing: ✓ Lower case ✓ Upper case ✓ Numbers ✓ Symbols

Time to crack your password:	**Review:** Fantastic, using that password makes you as secure as Fort Knox.
2 million years	

Your passwords are never stored. Even if they were, we have no idea who you are!

- **Kept secret.** Even the most unguessable password is easy to crack if it's written down.

- **Stored using reversible encryption**, so that the stored password can be decrypted when needed.

Q1 Brute force tactics are sometimes used by hackers to crack a password. What does this involve?

One way of making passwords more secure is to use a **password manager** to handle password creation, capture and replay. Users only need to remember a single master password or supply a unique biometric identification factor, such as a finger print, to access their password manager.

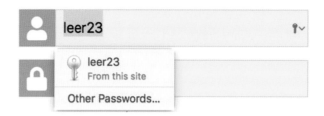

Password manager software:

- makes it easy for users to use long, complex, unique passwords across different sites and services without having to remember them or write them down
- can sync passwords across multiple devices
- prevents spyware or keystroke loggers from harvesting passwords

Two factor authentication

In order to protect themselves against ever more sophisticated attempts to gain unauthorised access, many organisations use more than one factor to establish someone's identity. Factors are:

- **what they know**, by providing a piece of knowledge, such as an ID, a password or a PIN
- **what they have**, by showing a physical artefact, such as an identity pass, a swipe card or an electronic key fob
- **who they are**, using a physical attribute such as their fingerprint, face or voice

Two factor authentication is an extra layer of security that commonly requires not only a password and username, but also one other from the list above to gain admittance.

To make gaining access even tougher, many organisations require employees to provide a third factor, so-called **multi-factor authentication**.

Someone attempting to gain unauthorised access may be able to meet two of the required criteria, but to meet all three would be very difficult.

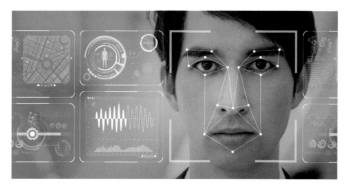

Biometrics

Biometric authentication is the process of identifying someone based on a physical attribute that is unique to them. The shape of their face, their fingerprints, retina, voice and DNA can all be used to verify their identity.

Biometrics offer several advantages over other forms of authentication.

- **Convenience.** There's no need for a user to carry any other form of identification or to remember any passwords.
- **Speed.** It's much quicker to present your face to a screen than it is to type in a complex password.
- **Security.** A user who falls victim to a phishing attack can't give their fingerprint away.

If a password gets stolen it can easily be changed, but a fingerprint or an iris is part of a person's identity and cannot be replaced.

Case study: Finding ways to beat biometrics

Hackers have already found ways to beat many of the current biometric solutions. In 2015 the fingerprint data of 5.6 million US federal employees was stolen.

The following year, Jan Krissler, a famous German hacker, known to fellow hackers as Starbug, used high-resolution photos of the hands of Ursula von der Leyen, Germany's Minister of Defence (pictured), to beat fingerprint authentication technology. He also got the better of Apple's TouchID technology just a day after its release by creating a copy of a fingerprint smudge left on an iPhone screen and using it to hack into the phone.

 What are the risks associated with biometric identification?

Using correct settings and levels of permitted access

One way an organisation can protect its digital systems and data from damage and theft is by applying the **principle of least privilege**. This gives employees only the bare minimum of permissions and administrative rights they need to do their job. Nothing more.

A low-level user will only be given access to a limited number of files and folders. Whereas, a super user will be able to access the most sensitive data on the system.

File permissions can be used to restrict what users can do with the content of file:

- **Read only:** Users can only read the contents of a file. They can't change its contents or delete it.
- **Read/write:** Users can read the contents of a file and add to it. They are not allowed to delete it.
- **Full access/full control:** Users can read a file, edit its contents and delete it.

Group or user names:

👥 Everyone	
👥 SYSTEM	

Add...   Remove

Permissions for Administrators	Allow	Deny	
Full control	☑	☐	⌃
Modify	☑	☐	
Read & execute	☑	☐	
List folder contents	☑	☐	
Read	☑	☐	⌄

A hacker who steals an employee's ID and password and gains entry to their user account will be restricted to those parts of the system and data that the employee has permission to access.

The more privileges the employee has, the more scope for malicious action the hacker will have.

Someone working in the sales department of a company, for example, would be given access to customer records, but not to the company payroll.

Similarly, if malware infects a user's computer, the malicious attack will be confined to the systems and data they have access to. Not too catastrophic if the user has limited access, but if they have high level permissions, there's nothing to stop the infection spreading system-wide.

Finding weaknesses and improving system security

If an organisation wants to improve the security of its systems and data, it first needs to know what it is doing wrong and where its weak spots are.

Ethical hacking and penetration testing

Contrary to popular belief, not all hackers are breaking the law. An **ethical hacker** works on behalf of an organisation, carrying out simulated hacking attacks on its digital systems to uncover any vulnerabilities that could be exploited by a criminal – a process known as **penetration testing**.

As well as looking for technical weaknesses, ethical hackers test out employees' security awareness, using a range of social engineering tactics to see how easily duped they are. They also provide advice on how to address any weaknesses they uncover.

Ethical hackers are often referred to as **white hat hackers** to differentiate them from **black hat hackers**, who operate with criminal intent.

Grey hat hackers occupy the middle ground. They don't have authorisation to attack an organisation's digital systems, but – instead of exploiting any loopholes they discover – they let the organisation know about them, though they do sometimes charge a fee, known as 'bug bounty', for doing so.

Case study: Grey hat hacker fixed routers without permission

In 2018, a mysterious Russian grey-hat hacker called Alexey claimed to have broken into over 100,000 routers and added firewall rules to their software so that they could no longer be exploited by crypto-miners and other criminals.

The routers were manufactured by a company in Latvia and were known to have security weaknesses. Alexey left a message for their owners telling them what he had done and offering to answer any questions they may have. He didn't get many thanks. Most people were annoyed that he had broken into their systems and made changes without their permission.

System and behaviour analysis

System behaviour analysis is the process of collecting and analysing information about activities that take place on a network – who logs on when and for how long, what files they access and what changes they make. Knowing what normal network usage looks like makes it easier to spot any unusual activity and enables IT staff to respond more quickly to an attack.

Exercises

1. GreenLeisure Limited is a holiday company offering a range of activities.

   (a) The company's network server is located at its head office. It is in a dedicated server room with secure access. Entry to the server room is currently controlled by an ID card system. The company wants to replace this with a biometric fingerprint scanning system.

   Explain **two** advantages of using a biometric access system rather than an ID card system. [4]

   (b) The company employs a number of instructors to run outdoor activities for holiday makers. They log on to the company network to find out how many people are booked onto each activity. Office staff handle customer bookings and payments.

   Explain **two** ways in which file permissions can be used to control how instructors and office staff access customer data. [4]

2. Manjit is an ethical hacker. She works for a well-respected security company.

   (a) Describe the role of an ethical hacker. [2]

   (b) Explain the difference between a 'grey hat hacker' and a 'white hat hacker'. [2]

   (c) One activity carried out by an ethical hacker is penetration testing.
   Describe what is meant by the term 'penetration testing'. [3]

3. Lawrence University is a major provider of higher education. More than 20,000 students attend lectures and tutorials on its campus. The university is carrying out a review of security.

   Discuss the security measures the university should take to control access to its facilities, digital systems and data. You should consider:

   • physical security measures
   • levels of permitted access
   • system and behaviour analysis [6]

Chapter 10
Data level protection

Objectives

- Understand measures used to protect and manage digital systems and data:
    - firewalls (hardware and software)
    - anti-virus software
    - device hardening
    - software/interface design (obscuring data entry, autocomplete, 'stay logged in')
    - encryption of stored data in individual files or whole drives
    - encryption of transmitted data

Data protection

An organisation has a legal obligation to keep personal data secure. Its competitiveness, possibly even its survival, may depend on keeping its business-critical data secret.

Unfortunately, there isn't a 'silver bullet' that is guaranteed to keep data safe. **Defence in depth** is the next best option. It involves using a combination of defence mechanisms. If an attacker breaks through one, they are confronted by another obstacle and then another. This delays their advance and gives the defender a chance to launch a counter-attack.

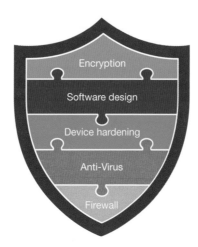

Firewall

A **firewall** is the first line of defence. The name firewall comes from the practice of placing a brick wall between two rooms, to prevent a fire in one room from spreading to the other.

A firewall acts as a barrier between an organisation's internal network and the Internet, monitoring incoming and outgoing traffic and using a pre-defined set of rules to determine what to allow through from one side to the other.

A **hardware firewall** is a physical device that filters traffic for an entire network. Typically, an organisation configures its firewall to allow incoming connections to port 80 – the standard port used by web servers. This enables people to visit its website, but denies access to traffic from unknown sources that tries to access any other port.

Sometimes two firewalls are deployed – one connected to the Internet and the other to the internal network. The public-facing web server is located between the two, in a so-called 'demilitarised zone'. This means that, even if an intruder succeeds in hacking into the web server, the second firewall will prevent them from accessing any other part of the network.

Multiple firewalls can be used to divide an organisation's internal network into separate segments. Should a worm or some other form of malware be unleashed, the infection is contained within a single segment and isn't able to spread across the whole network.

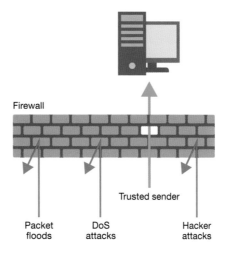

Firewall

Trusted sender

Packet
floods

DoS
attacks

Hacker
attacks

Firewalls do more than simply protect against external attacks. They can also flag up suspicious activity taking place on the internal network and prevent insiders from:

- downloading viruses whilst browsing online

- emailing sensitive data to themselves or to someone else outside

- visiting harmful or time-wasting websites

- downloading files from file sharing sites

A **software firewall** is a program installed on a computer to protect it against outside attempts to gain access to it. It works in a similar way to a hardware firewall. Many software firewalls have user-defined controls for setting up safe file and printer sharing and blocking installation of harmful applications. Some also incorporate privacy controls and web filtering. Most computer operating systems include a firewall, but third-party software firewalls are also available.

To provide maximum protection, an organisation should have a hardware firewall to protect its network and install a software firewall on each of its computers. It is especially important that any laptops that are taken off-site, where they aren't protected by the network firewall, have a software firewall installed.

Anti-virus software

Even with a firewall in place, an organisation's data is still vulnerable to attack. Malware poses a major threat. The purpose of **anti-virus (AV) software** is to detect and deal with malware, such as viruses, worms, Trojans, rootkits and spyware. It uses a combination of tactics to do so.

- **Signature-based detection** Every virus has unique program code (its signature). Anti-virus software saves a database of signatures, stored locally or in the cloud, which it compares with files on a computer's hard drive, or downloaded for example from the Internet or an email. It checks files before allowing them to be installed. If a match is found, the file is **quarantined** or deleted.

- **Quarantining** a file does not delete the file; instead, it puts it into a hidden folder that other programs cannot access. The deletion decision is left to the owner, who may send it to an anti-virus support team to investigate, if the file is really important.

- **Behavioural detection** keeps a lookout for any software that is behaving suspiciously – for example, executing automatically on start-up, downloading software from the Internet or encrypting files. This is one way an anti-virus software developer can detect new viruses and add their signatures to its database.

Some AV software also uses **machine learning** to help detect malicious software. It's ability to evolve and learn without human intervention enables it to respond much more rapidly to ever-changing threats.

> **Q1** Why should anti-virus software be configured to update automatically?

Device hardening

Although it is impossible to make a computer totally invulnerable, it is possible to 'toughen it up'. The objective of **device hardening** is to remove as many security risks as possible. A number of measures contribute to device hardening.

- **Installing a firewall and AV software** and keeping them up-to-date to fend off malware and hackers.

- **Using a password manager** that will ensure users choose strong passwords and eliminate the need for them to remember or write them down.

- **Keeping the operating system and application software up-to-date.** Hackers use known software vulnerabilities to gain unauthorised access to systems. To prevent this happening, updates and security patches should be applied as soon as they are released.

- **Removing unused software applications.** The more software there is installed on a computer, the more scope a hacker has to find and exploit vulnerabilities. Users can always ask for more software to be installed if they find they need it to do their job.

- **Removing redundant user accounts.** The fewer people who have access to a computer, the less chance a hacker has of acquiring useful login details.

- **Locking screens and automatically logging users out** if a computer is left unattended for more than a certain amount of time. This will help prevent unplanned, opportunist attacks.

- **Disabling USB ports** so that users can't copy sensitive data onto a portable storage device or install potentially harmful applications.

- **Enabling device auditing** so that computers can be monitored for unauthorised access attempts.

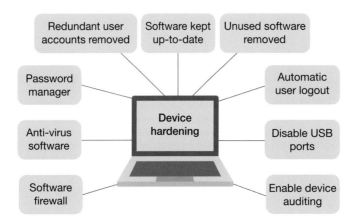

Every digital device belonging to an organisation should be hardened, including servers, desktop computers and laptops.

> Q2   **What measures should a user take to harden their own digital devices?**

Software/interface design

When it comes to security, humans are undoubtedly the weakest link. Software developers need to design software and interfaces with this in mind. Ease of use was once the key objective, but there is now a growing recognition of the need to balance usability with security.

- Intuitive interfaces. A simple solution, that is less dependent on user action to work, reduces the likelihood that users will make a mistake or carry out an action that could have security implications.
- Secure by default. Relying on users to make an application secure is not a good idea. It's much safer for security settings to be enabled by default.
- File encryption. Incorporating an encryption feature into software applications and operating systems makes it easier for the user to protect sensitive data.
- Avoiding auto-complete. An auto-complete option is understandably popular with users but has implications for security. It makes it easier for someone to gain access to an unattended computer.
- Two-factor authentication. Requiring users to provide additional authentication before allowing them to access systems containing sensitive data enhances security without necessarily making the experience less user-friendly. Biometric authentication, such as fingerprint or facial recognition, actually speeds up the process.
- Obscuring confidential data entry, such as passwords and account numbers, will prevent shoulder-surfers from gleaning any useful information.
- Automatically logging users out if they are inactive for any length of time will help thwart opportunists.

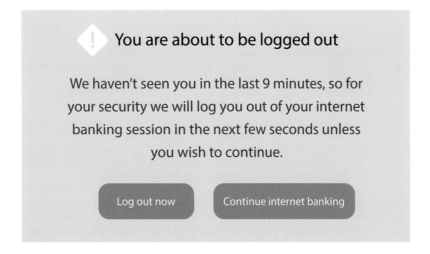

> Q3   The UK government is concerned about the security of Internet of Things (IoT) devices. It wants manufacturers to make their products 'secure by design'. How can they do this?

Encryption

Despite an organisation's best efforts, some data breaches will inevitably occur. But all is not lost; if the stolen data is encrypted, criminals won't be able to do anything with it.

Encryption is a technique for keeping data secure by only making it possible for authorised people to read it. It works by using a key to encode the data. Only someone in possession of the key is able to change the data back to its original form (decrypt it). Encrypted data is no use to a hacker. Even if they gain access to it, they won't be able to read it.

There are two types of encryption: symmetric and asymmetric. **Symmetric encryption** uses just one key to both encrypt and decrypt the data. If the key is discovered by a hacker, they can intercept the message without this being detected by sender or recipient.

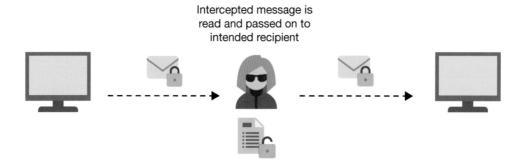

Intercepted message is read and passed on to intended recipient

Asymmetric encryption uses a pair of keys – a freely available public key to encrypt the data and a private key, known only to the recipient, to decrypt it.

It would take a hacker many years to crack encrypted data because complex mathematical algorithms and long numerical sequences are used to generate the keys. Encryption strength is directly related to key size. 256-bit encryption is stronger than 128-bit encryption.

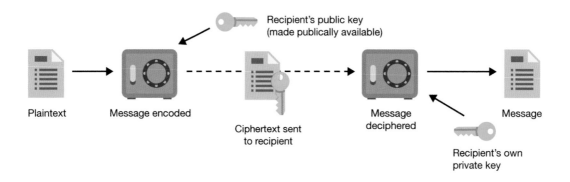

Recipient's public key (made publically available)

Plaintext　　Message encoded

Ciphertext sent to recipient

Message deciphered　　Message

Recipient's own private key

Q4　　**Some governments ban strong encryption. Why do you think they do this?**

Symmetric encryption is much faster and more efficient than asymmetric encryption but less secure. In practice, the two are often used in combination. Asymmetric encryption is used to exchange the key to be used securely and symmetric encryption to encrypt the data.

Organisations use encryption to protect their **stored data**.

- Individual files can be encrypted.

- Most operating systems have full-disk encryption built-in. This is particularly useful for protecting data stored on mobile phones and laptops.

- Some databases can be configured to store data in encrypted form.

Encryption is also used to protect **transmitted data** from interception by a third party. The data is encrypted before being sent and only converted back into a readable form when it reaches its destination. If a hacker manages to intercept the data whilst it is in transit, they won't be able to read it.

Encryption is widely used on the Internet to protect data being sent between a browser and a server. The letters '**https:**' at the start of a web address denotes that a website uses a secure connection. Organisations use secure, encrypted channels to communicate with customers and suppliers over the web.

 Q5 How does HTTPS provide increased security?

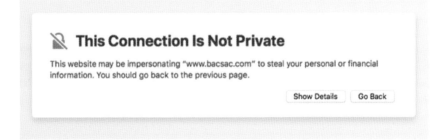

Exercises

1. Conor uses a laptop to carry out work-related activities.

    (a) Explain how anti-virus software will protect data stored on Conor's laptop.   [4]

    (b) The laptop has a software firewall installed. When Conor goes into the office he plugs his laptop into the company network. The network is protected by a hardware firewall.

    Explain how the hardware and software firewalls work together to enhance data security.   [3]

2. Installing a firewall is one device hardening technique.

    (a) State the purpose of device hardening.   [1]

    (b) Explain **three** other device hardening techniques.   [6]

3. Explain how encrypting data during transmission protects it from being read by an unauthorised person who intercepts the transmission.   [2]

4. This table lists five tools used to protect and manage digital systems and data.

    Complete the table. The first row has been done for you.

Function	Firewall	Anti-virus software	Device hardening	Software / interface design	Encryption
Detects malware using a database of signatures		✓			
Protects data from being read during transmission					
Prevents a virus from spreading across a network by dividing the network into segments					
A series of measures designed to make computers less vulnerable to attack					
Prevents employees from visiting malicious websites					
Quarantines suspicious files					
Reduces the security risk posed by users					

[6]

Chapter 11
Policy, backups and data recovery

Objectives

- Be able to define who is responsible for cyber security and policy and how concerns are reported
- Define security parameters including:
  - o Password policy
  - o Acceptable software/installation/usage policy
  - o Parameters for device hardening
- Understand the requirements of a disaster recovery policy including backup and recovery
- Understand the actions to take after an attack

The need for and nature of security policies

Unless organisations define what constitutes acceptable use of their digital systems and data, they can't expect staff to act responsibly. It is essential to have a set of security policies in place to spell out exactly what is permitted and how employees are expected to behave.

A **policy** is an official written statement that defines a way of doing something or a plan of action. An organisation's security policy will make it clear:

- who can access a specific resource – a file, storage device, database or computer – and what they are allowed to do with it
- what sort of password employees must set and what they must do (or not do) to keep it safe
- how, where and when data will be backed up
- the procedures that must be followed, in the event of disruption, to get systems up and running and restore data as quickly as possible

A policy will only be effective if everyone knows that it exists and is familiar with the contents.

Many organisations require their staff to sign a copy of their security policy to confirm that they have read and agreed to adhere to it.

Of course, it's no good having a policy if no disciplinary action is taken against anyone who flouts it. Organisations must enforce their security policies if they want them to be effective.

Acceptable Use Agreement

I have read and understood the Acceptable Use Policy, and will abide by it when using computers and accessing data.

I further understand that any violation of the **organisation's policies and procedures** is unethical and may constitute a criminal offence. Should I commit any violation, my access may be revoked and/or legal action initiated.

User Signature: *Damian Lee*

 Q1 Apart from employees, who else may sometimes read an organisation's security policy?

Defining responsibilities

Roles and responsibilities

Overall responsibility for information security within an organisation rests with a senior member of staff; usually the Managing Director.

The IT Director or a designated **Information Security Manager** is responsible for writing and implementing security policies.

A **Data Protection Officer** will advise on data protection laws and best practice.

In a small or medium sized organisation, all these roles may be carried out by the same person.

All employees have a duty to adhere to the policies and report any suspected breach in security to the Information Security Manager.

Reporting

Many organisations have a **whistleblowing policy** so that employees can raise concerns without fear of victimisation or dismissal. It sets out the procedure to follow if an employee thinks that a colleague is behaving suspiciously or being irresponsible, or indeed if the organisation itself is doing something that puts personal data at risk.

Awareness raising campaigns, information and training help employees to become more security-conscious and more willing to report concerns.

Some Information Security Managers produce regular threat reports, detailing the attacks they have encountered and flagging up any new ones that are likely to occur. This helps to raise awareness across the organisation and make everyone more vigilant.

Defining security parameters

A **security parameter** establishes or restricts how something must be done. Organisations must set security parameters for activities such as password creation and protection, software installation and usage, acceptable use of its systems and device hardening.

Password policy

A poorly chosen or unprotected password puts an organisation's digital systems and data at risk.

The purpose of a **password policy** is to ensure that:

- only strong passwords are used
- passwords are changed regularly
- passwords are kept safe and not disclosed to others
- employees are aware of the risks, know what is required of them and understand how the policy will be monitored and enforced

---

Password Policy

This policy applies to all employees and contractors of A&B Enterprises and governs acceptable password use on all systems that connect to the company's network or access its data.

Password creation

- All user passwords must be at least 8 characters in length.
- Password dictionaries should be utilised to prevent the use of common and easily cracked passwords.
- Passwords must be completely unique, and not used for any other system, application, or personal account.
- Default installation passwords must be changed immediately after installation is complete.
- Passwords must be changed every 3 months. Previously used passwords may not be reused.

Password Protection

- Passwords must not be shared with anyone
- Passwords must not be written down.
- User IDs and passwords must not be scripted to enable automatic login.
- 'Remember Password' features on websites and applications should not be used.
- All mobile devices that connect to the company network must be secured with a password and biometric authentication and must be configured to lock after 3 minutes of inactivity.

It is your responsibility to adhere to the rules set out in this policy.

If you believe your password may have been compromised, please report the incident IMMEDIATELY to Andrea Hill and change the password.

Acceptable use policy

An **acceptable use policy** stipulates how employees are expected to behave when using an organisation's digital systems and data and what they are not permitted to do. It also defines the sanctions that will be imposed if unacceptable behaviour occurs.

Appropriate behaviour, such as:

- encrypting sensitive or confidential information stored on a laptop
- not leaving a computer unattended without logging off from the network
- keeping an eye out for shoulder surfers

Prohibited activities, such as:

- visiting online gambling or pornography websites
- downloading files from the Internet
- installing unapproved software
- sending emails that disclose confidential information

You can read more about acceptable use policies in Chapter 15.

 Q2 How effective do you think an organisation's acceptable use policy is in influencing employees' online behaviour?

Parameters for device hardening

Device hardening parameters specify how an organisation's computers must be set up and configured so as to make them as secure as possible. Measures will include:

- applying all appropriate security patches and firmware updates
- removing any unnecessary software and drivers
- installing a firewall and anti-virus software
- configuring default security settings
- encrypting the hard drives of any computers containing sensitive information.

Disaster recovery policy

A surprising number of organisations – particularly small ones – seem to believe that they are immune to disaster. When things go wrong, they are totally unprepared. Many go out of business as a result.

A **disaster** is a sudden event, such as a malware infection, a ransomware attack, a system failure, a fire, or theft of data, that seriously disrupts the function of an organisation.

The purpose of a **disaster recovery policy** is to provide a detailed plan for responding to a disaster. It sets out:

- who is responsible for doing what
- procedures for backing up and recovering data
- who needs to be informed and how that will be done

Having a disaster recovery policy in place helps an organisation to deal promptly with problems when they occur, get back up and running quickly and meet its legal obligations.

Roles and responsibilities

A team of people will be needed to carry out the recovery plan. A team leader will be responsible for setting the plan in motion, coordinating the work of team members and resolving any problems they encounter along the way.

All employees will need to be informed of the situation and how it affects them. It may be that systems are down for a while, preventing them from doing any work. They will need to know what to say and what not to say when dealing with customers, suppliers or members of the press.

Backup and recovery

Backup and recovery procedures describe the process of creating and storing backup copies in a separate system or medium, so as to protect against the possibility of data loss.

RAID is a commonly used approach. RAID stands for 'Redundant Array of Independent Disks'. Each hard disk on a server is replicated on a second disk. Should one disk fail, the other one springs into action, allowing the failed disk to be swapped out without the server having to be shut down.

RAID provides good protection against hard disk failures, but won't protect data in the event of a fire in the server room or a malicious physical attack on the building in which the server is located. Nor will RAID help if the server is infected by malware. For this reason, organisations keep backups of their data off-site. Nowadays, many back up their data to the cloud.

 Why do many organisations back up their data to the cloud instead of having their own backup facilities on-site?

A backup and recovery plan will specify:

- the process for backing up data – what is backed up, how often, on what storage medium
- the procedure for recovering data from backup
- arrangements for relocating staff and computer equipment to an alternative site if necessary
- how alternative premises and stand-by IT equipment are to be maintained and tested in readiness to take over in the event of an emergency
- the time frame in which systems must be up and running and data recovered following a disaster

Actions to take during and after an attack

The disaster recovery team must spring into action as soon as an attack is discovered. They will carry out a pre-determined five stage plan.

Investigate. The team must establish what type of attack is underway and how much disruption it is causing or is likely to cause.

Respond. If personal data has been compromised, the Information Commissioner's Office (ICO) must be notified within seven days. All those affected must be contacted. The police must be informed if a crime is thought to have taken place. Shareholders, suppliers, business partners and other stakeholders must be briefed.

Manage. Appropriate procedures must be implemented to contain the attack. This may require systems to be shut down.

Recover. Once the attack is over, any data that has been destroyed, encrypted or compromised, will need to be restored from backups. Any equipment that has been damaged will need to be replaced. If the attackers exploited previously unknown security vulnerabilities to carry out an attack, these must be located and patched.

Analyse. Once everything is up and running again, the team will need to establish exactly what happened and how it could have been prevented. Policies and procedures may need to be revised and additional staff training provided.

Exercises

1. CleverTech develop Internet of Things (IoT) devices for the home.

   (a) Describe **two** ways in which the company can make its staff more security-conscious. [4]

   (b) Anya works in the marketing department. She has found a free image editor on a website and installed it on her company laptop.

   Describe how an organisation's security policies would prevent this sort of behaviour. [2]

   (c) The company has a password policy. One rule of the policy is that passwords must be changed every three months.

   Explain **two** other rules that would increase the security of passwords. [4]

2. Mina is the Information Security Manager of a large hospital.

   Discuss the issues she should consider when deciding on procedures for backup and recovery. [6]

3. A secondary school has fallen victim to a ransomware attack. All the students' GCSE coursework has been encrypted. The malware found its way onto the school's network because a teacher failed to recognise a phishing email.

   (a) Explain what is meant by the term 'phishing'. [2]

   (b) Describe how an acceptable use policy might have prevented a successful phishing attack. [3]

LEARNING AIM C
Wider implications of digital systems

In this section:

Chapter 12
Shared data

Objectives

- Understand how data is shared, including:
  - location-based data
  - transactional data
  - cookies
  - data exchange between services
- Understand the benefits and drawbacks of using shared data
- Understand the responsible use of data including:
  - legal considerations
  - privacy
  - ethical use

Shared data

Even before computers were invented, people generated and stored a lot of data – records of financial transactions, movement of goods, births, marriages, deaths, school reports or recipes for example.

The emergence of digital systems in the second half of the 20th century has brought about an explosion in the amount of data being generated. It is estimated that, by 2025, the world will be producing around 160 zettabytes of data a year. (A **zettabyte** is one trillion gigabytes.)

Every time someone carries out a digital action they leave behind a **digital footprint**. Digital footprints can be active or passive.

When someone intentionally shares data about themselves with others, by for example posting an image on social media, they create an **active digital footprint**.

People unintentionally (and often unknowingly) leave behind **passive digital footprints** when carrying out day-to-day activities, such as getting cash out of an ATM, using Google Maps to get directions, donating to charity, accessing healthcare or using public transport.

An individual's digital footprints say a lot about them. Third parties, such as advertisers, health professionals, planners, prospective employers and law enforcement agencies, are eager to tap into this valuable source of information.

Q1   What are the pros and cons of third parties having access to someone's digital footprint?

The amount of **machine-generated data** is also growing rapidly. Machines in factories are equipped with sensors that gather and transmit data. Data is generated when 'smart' home devices communicate with each other and with external devices. Embedded systems built into vehicles are constantly churning out a stream of real-time data.

Data consists of raw, unorganised facts. It only becomes useful information when it is structured, analysed and put into context. Fortunately, not only does digital technology enable us to generate large quantities of data, it also provides us with the means to store and process it.

Location-based data

Real-time location-based data is generated by mobile digital devices, such as mobile phones, fitness trackers, augmented reality headsets and vehicle navigation systems.

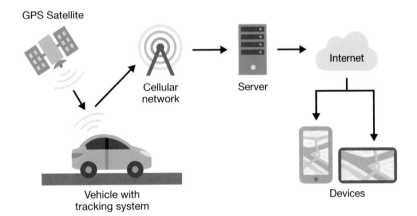

A GPS (Global Positioning System) receiver inside a digital device scans for and then locks onto signals from satellites orbiting the earth. There over 30 of them in total, positioned so that at least four are visible to a GPS-enabled device at any given time. By measuring the distance from itself to each satellite it finds, the receiver can pinpoint its position.

A GPS receiver isn't always able to pick up satellite signals in built-up urban areas or inside buildings. To get around this problem, a combination of GPS, Wi-Fi and cellular communication technologies is used.

> **Case study:** Google Maps Navigation
>
> Google's map services provide users with their own location information using data from satellites. This, combined with Google's satellite imagery of Earth, is used to place the user's location on a recognisable map. Turn-by-turn navigation is also used to provide directions from one place to another. Live traffic information is displayed by using the speed and location data from other Android devices accessing Google Maps.

A growing number of systems and services make use of location-based data.

- **Taxi services**, like Uber, use it to pair customers with nearby taxis.
- **Airports, railway and bus stations** use it to provide accurate arrival times.

- **Fitness trackers** use it to track when and where a user is exercising.
- **Retailers** use it to help their customers locate the store nearest them, choose a convenient pickup point and find out when their goods will be delivered.

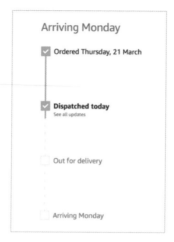

- **Satnavs** use it to provide directions, alternative routes, speed camera alerts and information about places of interest nearby.
- **Messaging apps** use it to add geotags to posts.
- **Location-based augmented reality games**, such as Pokémon GO, use it to place digital overlays over actual physical surroundings.
- **Advertisers** use it to send people notifications of offers and promotions close to where they are.
- **The probation service** uses it to keep track of offenders when they are released from prison.

The main benefit of location-based data for individuals is convenience, but there are drawbacks. Friends aren't the only ones who get to know someone's whereabouts. Location-based data makes it easy for criminals to locate potential victims.

 Personal tracking systems are used to track people's movements.

What are the pros and cons of using location-based data for this purpose?

Transactional data

A **transaction** is an exchange between organisations and/or individuals. Activities, such as purchasing a product or service, reserving a table at a restaurant, subscribing to an online service or filling out a form all generate transactional data.

Imagine a couple doing the weekly shop at their local supermarket. When they reach the checkout with their trolley full of goods, the transaction produces a lot of data such as:

- the name and location of the supermarket they are in
- the id of the checkout they are using
- the date and time of the purchase
- the product code, name and price of each item
- which vouchers they redeem and how much they are worth
- the total amount owed

- the method of payment selected and – if they opt to pay by card – the card number
- their loyalty card number
- how many plastic bags they request/buy

By analysing transactional data, supermarkets gain valuable insights into their customers' shopping habits, likes and dislikes. This enables them to offer a more personalised service, for example issuing customers with vouchers and special offers for things they like to buy.

Supermarkets are just one of many organisations that make use of transactional data but not everybody is happy that their data is being used in this way. Many people do not like being kept in the dark about who has access to it, what it is being used for and who it is passed on to. They are concerned that poor security could result in criminals getting hold of their data, making them vulnerable to identity theft and fraud.

Identity theft involves stealing someone else's personal details, such as their bank account number, sort code or passport number. These details can be used to make purchases, running up debts in the real owner's name.

 Q3 A supermarket collects and analyses sales data to find out more about its customers.

What other intelligence could be gleaned from this data and how could it be used?

Cookies

A **cookie** is a small text file that is downloaded onto a user's computer when they visit a website. It enables the website to recognise the user's device and store information about their preferences or past actions.

There are two types of cookie. A **session cookie** exists only whilst someone is visiting a site and is removed when they leave. Session cookies are used to store the data that is generated as a visitor moves from page to page. Online stores, for example, use session cookies to keep details of items customers place in their shopping basket prior to checking out.

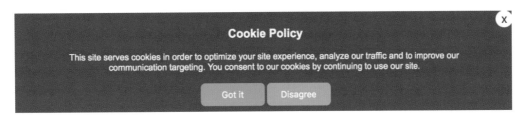

A **persistent cookie** remains on a user's computer even after they have left the site and have finished browsing. Using persistent cookies means the user doesn't need to login or re-enter their preferences or other information.

Cookies make browsing the web more convenient for users. Once registered on a shopping site like Amazon, for example, they don't have to re-enter the same information on each subsequent visit. Websites can tailor content to their known preferences.

Many people enjoy the personalised recommendations that cookies enable online stores, such as Amazon, to provide. The drawback is that data stored in cookies reveals personal information about them that they may prefer to keep to themselves.

Data exchange between services

Instead of keeping their data strictly within their organisation and not allowing anyone else to access it, some organisations have begun to recognise the benefits of sharing what they have with others. Pooling their data helps them to make better decisions and deliver more targeted services.

- By linking household benefits data with social service records, local authorities can more easily identify children at risk and intervene sooner to protect them.

- By bringing together data about a patient's medical history, lifestyle and DNA, healthcare professionals can tailor treatment to meet an individual's specific needs.

- By combining information from embedded sensors with location data, traffic managers can monitor congestion and direct drivers to alternative routes to prevent traffic building up.

- By harnessing and analysing shared data, police forces are able to deter criminals and prevent terrorists from carrying out attacks.

- By combining data from observatories all over the word, scientists have been able to create a 'virtual' radio telescope the size of Earth and produce an image of a black hole for the first time.

Benefits and drawbacks of using shared data

	Benefits
Individuals	**Personalisation.** Individuals get recommendations, products and services that are tailored to their preferences and location.
	Convenience. It's quick and easy to access the goods and services they are interested in. Personal details, such as credit card number and address, only have to be entered once.
Organisations	**Informed decision making.** By analysing shared data, organisations gain a deeper insight into their customers, enabling them to provide products and services that meet their needs. This leads to increased sales.
	Improved efficiency. By analysing operational data, organisations can improve their efficiency and cut costs.

	Drawbacks
Individuals	**Privacy.** Individuals don't always know who is analysing their data, what they are using it for or who else it is being passed onto. Conclusions drawn from analysis of the data may be wrong. The data itself may be inaccurate or out-of-date.
	Security. Organisations have a poor track record of keeping data secure. If shared data falls into the wrong hands it might be misused.
	Discrimination. Analysis of shared data could result in some groups or individuals being discriminated against. For example, people with a known family history of cancer could be refused life insurance or have to pay more than the normal rate for it.
	Civil liberties. Analysis of shared data by police forces could wrongly associate innocent people with criminal behaviour or categorise people according to their political views.
Organisations	**Reputation.** Organisations are legally bound to keep personal data secure. An organisation's reputation will be seriously damaged if it fails to keep personal data secure.
	Non-compliance. If poor security results in a data breach, organisations will face prosecution, hefty fines and claims for compensation.
	Data quality. The decisions organisations make are only as good as the intelligence on which they are based. Poor quality data may lead them to misjudge customers' needs.

Analysis of large volumes of shared data can have significant benefits for society.

- Data analysis saved lives by helping aid workers prioritise relief efforts after Typhoon Haiyan devastated the Philippines in 2013.
- The Clinton Health Access Initiative uses medical data to forecast demand for HIV/AIDS, malaria and tuberculosis drugs, so as to ensure that enough are manufactured and available when and where they are needed.
- Conservationists analyse camera-trap images and location-based data to track the movement of poaching gangs in parts of Africa to prevent them from harming endangered animals.
- In April 2018, Baroness Tessa Jowell became the first person to donate her medical data to a new global database, the Universal Cancer Databank. If millions of cancer sufferers around the world share their data, researchers are confident that they will be able to eliminate cancer.

Responsible use

Organisations that collect and use personal data have a responsibility to comply with data protection legislation and are accountable for how they handle personal data.

Legal considerations, privacy and ethical use

The **Data Protection Act 2018** stipulates what data organisations can legally collect and what they are allowed to do with it.

The **Privacy and Electronic Communications Regulations 2003** govern how cookies can be used.

You can read more about these laws in Chapter 16.

Individuals are beginning to understand the value of their data. Trust and transparency are important considerations when deciding what personal data to share.

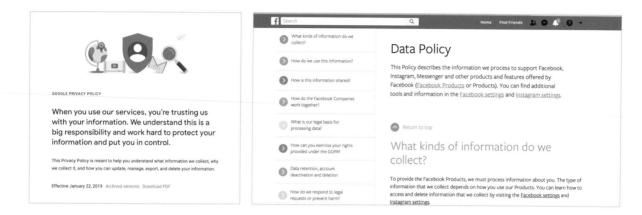

Many organisations are responding by publishing a data policy that explains clearly what they will and won't do with an individual's data, enabling consumers to make more informed decisions about which services to use or products to buy.

Exercises

1. (a) Joe's mobile phone tracks his location.

    (i) Describe **two** potential advantages to Joe of this technology. [4]

    (ii) Explain how the use of location-based data could impact on Joe's privacy. [2]

   (b) Joe wants to buy a new laptop. When he visits an online store, transactional data is collected.

    (i) Give **two** examples of transactional data the store could collect. [2]

    (ii) Online stores value transactional data.

    Explain **one** reason why this is the case. [2]

2. Green Leisure is a holiday company based in the Peak District.

   (a) The company's website uses cookies.

   State **three** purposes of using cookies. [3]

   (b) Websites must obtain 'informed consent' from visitors before using cookies.

   Explain why this is necessary. [3]

3. Layla makes an appointment to see a doctor. The doctor's surgery exchanges data with the hospital and the pharmacy.

   Explain **two** ways in which this data exchange benefits Layla. [4]

4. Anke frequently travels long distances for work and is often away overnight. She is a member of a hotel rewards scheme and earns points when she stays overnight at any participating hotel.

   Discuss the benefits and drawbacks to the hotel chain of operating such a scheme. [6]

Chapter 13
Environmental issues

Objectives

- Understand the impact of manufacture, use and disposal of IT systems on the environment
- Evaluate the environmental considerations when upgrading or replacing computers
- Explain the energy saving settings and policies available for digital devices

Manufacture, use and disposal

Around a million new Internet users come online every day. More than five billion people have a mobile phone. Many people in the UK and elsewhere own more than one digital device.

The manufacture, use and disposal of all this IT equipment has a significant impact on the environment.

Manufacture

Large quantities of raw materials are used in the manufacture of digital devices. Many, like copper, gold and palladium, are non-renewable and rare. A **non-renewable** material is a natural resource which, once used up, cannot be replaced. Some, like arsenic, cadmium and chromium, are highly toxic. 97% of the rare-earth metals used in the manufacturing process are mined in China, which has comparatively low environmental protection standards.

Mining activities are often dangerous and poorly regulated. Excavation causes extensive damage to the local environment, scarring the landscape with unsightly waste heaps, contaminating water supplies and damaging wildlife habitats.

Once extracted, raw materials are shipped to factories to be manufactured into components such as circuit boards, chips, screens, disk drives and cases. The manufacturing process is energy-intensive, using large amounts of non-renewable fossil fuels such as coal and oil. Burning fossil fuels produces carbon dioxide (CO_2) and contributes to global warming.

A large volume of water is also required. It takes around 2000 gallons of water to create just one computer chip. Chemical-polluted waste water is a bi-product of the process and can cause environmental damage if it is not handled carefully.

In the UK, the restriction on the use of certain hazardous substances (ROHS regulations 2012) used in the manufacture of electrical and electronic equipment, such as digital devices, encouraged manufacturers to use more environmentally-friendly alternatives. Unfortunately, some have responded by simply moving their production processes overseas to countries where environmental regulations are not so strict.

Transportation of raw materials, components and finished goods, often over huge distances, also impacts on the environment. A lot of packaging waste ends up in the oceans, with plastic being a major cause of concern.

Use

Keeping the world's IT systems and devices up and running, day in day out, requires a lot of electricity. A PC that is on for eight hours a day uses almost 600 kWh of electricity per year. A laptop uses around half that amount and a mobile phone considerably less.

Every Internet activity, from streaming a video to posting a comment on Facebook, requires huge amounts of data to be stored. Data centres are springing up all over the world and the amount of energy they consume is predicted to treble over the next ten years, putting a massive strain on energy supplies.

 Q1 Bitcoin mining involves using your computer power to solve complicated logic problems. It is extremely energy-intensive. Why is this the case and what is its impact on the environment?

Case study: Facebook's eco-friendly data centre

Facebook has built a huge data centre in Lulea, northern Sweden, just 100km south of the Arctic Circle. Expansion plans announced in 2018 are set to make it one of the largest data centres in the world. The location was selected because of its access to renewable hydroelectricity and its cold climate, which helps to keep the servers cool. German car maker, BMW, also stores data in the region.

Disposal

Any form of discarded electronic equipment, including computers, printers and other digital devices, is referred to as **e-waste**.

With so many new devices being manufactured each year, it's not surprising that approximately 50 million tons of e-waste is produced each year. Although it contains valuable and reusable materials, such as metals and rare earth elements, only around 20% of e-waste is currently recycled.

Developing countries, such as Nigeria and Pakistan, are willing to import e-waste for a fee. Once there, it often gets dumped in landfill sites. Over time, toxic substances in e-waste may leak into the ground, contaminating water supplies and posing a long-term health risk.

Q2   **Research safer ways to recycle old computers.**

Even recycling is not without problems. The quickest and most common way of separating e-waste into raw materials is to burn it, but this releases harmful chemicals into the atmosphere.

In the UK, the **Waste Electrical and Electronic Equipment Regulations (WEEE) 2018** set targets for the collection, recycling and recovery of electronic equipment. Manufacturers are required to operate a recycling programme to recover recyclable materials and dispose of dangerous substances safely. Some take old devices in part payment for new models.

Unwanted digital devices can be donated to charities, like Computer Aid, that provides refurbished IT equipment to schools, universities and other institutions in Europe, South America and Africa.

Upgrade or replace

Having the latest digital technology is a status symbol. This motivates many people to replace devices much sooner than they need to. The life cycle of a mobile phone in the UK is less than two years. Companies such as Samsung and Apple know this and frequently introduce new devices and new models of existing devices.

In the UK, around a quarter of the digital devices thrown away still work or would do so if minor repairs were made. Lots of people have old, unused mobile phones and tablets kept at home, even though someone else would be able to make good use of them.

There are no hard-and-fast rules about when to upgrade a digital device and when it is best to replace it. Generally, the longer it is kept in action, the better it is for the environment.

However, upgrading is not always straightforward. Desktop computers can be opened up reasonably easily to add more memory or replace a hard drive, but mobile devices have sealed cases that can't be easily opened. This makes it difficult to undertake 'do-it-yourself' repairs or upgrades, and sending devices back to the manufacturer is expensive.

Some digital devices may still work, but are rendered obsolete because manufacturers stop providing security updates for them or because they can no longer run the latest software updates.

 Q3 Access to repair needs to be cheaper and easier. What else should be done to prolong the life of a digital device?

When the time comes to replace a device, instead of buying the latest model, consumers could opt for a refurbished or used alternative. That said, newer models are generally more energy efficient than older ones.

They could pass on their old device to a recycling company or a charity, rather than throwing it away or stowing it at the back of a drawer.

Usage and settings policies

In recent years, considerable efforts have been made to improve the energy efficiency of digital devices. The amount of energy they consume depends on how they are used and what they are used for. Software to carry out complex calculations, 3D modelling and video games is particularly power hungry.

There are various ways to reduce the energy consumption of digital devices.

- A **power saving mode** can be activated so that the device shuts down or goes to sleep when not in use.
- **Wi-Fi, Bluetooth and GPS** can be switched off when not in use so that they don't needlessly continue to emit signals.
- **Dormant applications** can be closed down so that they don't continue to run in the background.
- **Peripherals**, such as printers, speakers and external drives can be turned off when they are not being used.

- The **brightness of the screen** can be reduced. The default setting is often very high and can be lowered without it making any discernible difference.

Hardcopy versus electronic distribution

Some people argue that electronic distribution of documents, newspapers, magazines or books for example is better for the environment than producing written letters or printed copies of brochures.

In reality, each has an environmental impact. Electronic distribution cuts down on paper usage and consequently the number of trees that have to be felled, but consumes more energy. It's up to consumers to decide responsibly which format to use for what.

Exercises

1. Describe **three** ways in which IT systems are harmful to the environment. [6]

2. Maddie buys a new tablet. She wants to recycle her old one.
    (a) State **two** environmentally friendly ways in which Maddie could dispose of her old tablet. [2]
    (b) Describe **two** other ways in which the impact of IT systems on the environment can be reduced. [4]

3. WeStore is a cloud storage provider. The company is planning to build a new data centre.
    Describe how it can reduce the environmental impact of the data centre. [3]

4. A furniture company is going to produce a brochure of its products.
    Discuss the environmental impact of hard (paper) copy versus electronic distribution. [6]

Chapter 14
Equal access

Objectives

- Understand the importance of providing equal access to digital services and information:
  - benefits to organisations, individuals and society
  - legal requirements
  - professional guidelines / accepted standards

- Understand net neutrality and its impact on organisations

Equal access to services and information

With just a couple of clicks, people can buy what they want and get it delivered to their door, submit a tax return, find out about an apprenticeship, enrol on a course, stream the latest film, check their eligibility for benefits and much more besides. Digital technology enables individuals to access services and information quickly and easily. However, not everyone is able to take advantage of what technology has to offer.

Digital exclusion is the inability to access online information or services or to use digital devices. Factors such as poor connectivity, old age, disability, poverty, low income and lack of digital skills, all contribute to digital exclusion.

The **digital divide** is the gap between people who do not have access to digital technology and those who do.

Around 11 million adults in the UK do not have sufficient digital skills to perform everyday activities, such as going online, sending an email, filling in an online form or making an online payment. Nor do they know how to use a mobile phone or a laptop.

Elsewhere, around 50% of the world's population do not have Internet access. In addition, there are huge disparities in connection speeds between countries.

Digitally excluded people:

- are unable to take advantage of education and training opportunities available online
- are more likely to suffer from social isolation or loneliness
- pay more for goods and services because they can't shop around online for good deals
- can only get poorly paid jobs and are at risk of falling into poverty
- are unable to access online public services
- miss out on streaming services and other forms of online entertainment

It's not just individuals who benefit from equal access. Organisations need people with good digital skills to fill their job vacancies and enable them to take advantage of the opportunities technology provides to operate more efficiently, grow their business and embrace new ways of working.

The distribution of wealth in the world is already uneven. Access – or lack of it – to digital technology and the Internet is unbalancing the situation still further. Countries with large numbers of Internet users are becoming richer, while those with relatively few are becoming even poorer in comparison.

Benefits of equal access

	Benefits of providing equal access
Organisations	**Skilled workforce.** The pool of skilled labour from which to recruit is bigger, making it easier for organisations to fill vacancies for jobs that require good digital skills. Having a digitally savvy workforce enables them to embrace new ways of working, such as cloud services, online meetings and remote working.
	Improved productivity. Equipped with good digital skills, employees are able to work more efficiently and improve their productivity.
	Competitive edge. In the next two decades, it is estimated that 90% of jobs will require some form of digital skills. Having a workforce with good digital skills will help organisations stay competitive.
	Increased revenue. With more people in work and incomes rising, organisations have an opportunity to attract new customers, sell more products and services and make more money.
Individuals	**Information and services.** Being able to go online gives people access to entertainment, education, employment etc. irrespective of where they live.
	Employment and earnings. People with good digital skills find it easier to get work, have better jobs opportunities and earn more money. They may be able negotiate a flexible working arrangement or improve their work/life balance. They are able to access online education and training to improve their skillset further.
	Cost saving. Having the skills to use the Internet to compare prices and shop online gives people more choice and helps them save money. Being able to use online banking helps them avoid getting into debt and paying overdraft fees.
	Time saving. Being able to complete transactions online is usually quicker than having to visit a bank branch or local council office.
	Social isolation. By using social media, email etc. people can keep in touch with friends, family and their local community, helping them to feel more connected.
Society	**Tax revenues.** With more people in work, tax revenues will increase.
	Democracy. Digital technology gives more people a voice on the issues that affect them and makes for a more open society.
	Public services. The more people who can access government services online, the more the burden on public services, such as the NHS, is reduced. Uptake of services, such as the NHS Website and e-prescriptions, will reduce the number of avoidable GP visits.

In 2017 the UK published a Digital Strategy designed to ensure that everyone in the country has the necessary digital skills to fully participate in society.

 Q1 Apart from upskilling people, what else needs to be done in the UK to achieve full participation?

Barriers to digital inclusion

Achieving full participation requires a number of challenges to be overcome.

Infrastructure. Despite significant investment, there are still some areas of the UK where households don't have Internet access at all or where Internet speeds are unacceptably slow. Rural areas are particularly disadvantaged. Mobile phone coverage is improving but 3G – let alone 4G – still isn't available everywhere.

The **Digital Economy Act 2017** guarantees the right of all UK residents to a minimum standard of broadband connectivity – one that delivers download speeds of 10 Mbps. Consumers are entitled to receive automatic compensation when their broadband services are below this minimum standard.

Many parts of the world don't have a reliable electricity supply or adequate telecommunications infrastructure.

Case study: Improving connectivity in developing countries

Alphabet, (who own Google) has launched a project in India that uses light beams to deliver high-speed, high-capacity connectivity to bring the Internet to rural areas. It has also been trialling an initiative called Project Loon, that involves maintaining a fleet of balloons to provide Internet coverage to remote regions.

OneWeb, a company backed by Richard Branson and Elon Musk's SpaceX are placing satellites in low Earth orbit to provide fast Internet access.

Case study: Affordable computers

getonline@home is a UK charity that sells heavily discounted, refurbished Internet-ready computers and tablets to people in receipt of benefits, registered charities and the disabled.

IT Schools Africa supplies good quality refurbished digital devices to schools in several African countries.

Cost. People with less disposable income and the poorer countries of the world don't have a great deal of money to spend on digital devices and Internet connectivity. Various charities exist that aim to overcome this barrier by providing affordable technology to those who need it.

Lack of skills. A £400,000 Digital Inclusion Fund has been launched by the UK government to help older and disabled people learn how to book GP appointments online, use a search engine and use apps to communicate with friends and family.

Ambitious training programmes are underway in India, Kenya, Columbia and elsewhere to ensure that people there have the know-how and skills they need to exploit digital technology to the full.

Accessibility. Assistive technology such as voice recognition software, screen readers and alternative input devices enable people with mobility and sensory impairments to use digital devices.

Modern operating systems such as Windows and Mac OS include a number of accessibility features such as Voiceover, which provides spoken descriptions of items displayed on the screen, and Dictation, which allows users to talk instead of type.

Q2 What accessibility features are provided by an operating system to help people who are deaf or hard of hearing?

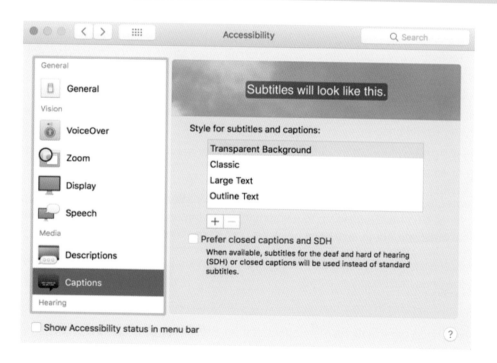

Legal requirements

The **Equality Act 2010** protects people against discrimination in the workplace and in wider society. Organisations are legally obliged to make 'reasonable adjustments' to enable disabled people to access the same opportunities and services as able-bodied people.

This means, for example, that an employer must provide special assistive technology, such as an adapted keyboard for someone with arthritis or a large screen for a visually impaired employee.

The Act also obliges website owners to make their sites accessible to disabled users. There are various things they can do to achieve this. See Chapter 5.

Professional guidelines / accepted standards

As well as the legislation, a whole raft of guidelines and standards spell out how organisations should behave and what they should do to promote equal access.

The World Wide Web Consortium (W3C) is the international body that defines standards for the web. It has published a set of guidelines for making websites more accessible.

The British Standards Institute (BSI) has a code of practice on web accessibility, aimed at helping organisations comply with the Equality Act 2010.

Net neutrality

Net neutrality is the principle that Internet service providers (ISPs) must allow all content and applications to access the Internet at the same speed, under the same conditions and without favouring or blocking particular sites or services.

Net neutrality impacts on organisations in a number of ways.

- It creates a level playing field. All organisations, irrespective of size, have exactly the same access to the Internet at the same price. This helps small companies and start-ups compete with large companies and encourages innovation.
- ISPs can't restrict heavy bandwidth services, such as video streaming, or slow down access to particular applications.
- ISPs aren't allowed to create Internet 'fast lanes' and charge more for using them. If they were able to do this, small organisations would be adversely affected and the large ones, who could afford to pay for a faster service, would become even more dominant.
- It prevents ISPs from charging more for access to popular services, such as online banking, video streaming or email.

Net neutrality is protected in the UK by the **Electronic Communications and Wireless Telegraphy Regulations 2011**. In addition, most ISPs have signed up to a voluntary open Internet code of practice, agreeing to provide full and open Internet access and not to restrict or block any data or services.

In the USA, legislation protecting net neutrality was repealed in 2018. Early indications are that small organisations are the ones most badly affected.

 Why are small organisations more affected than larger ones when net neutrality agreements are relaxed?

Exercises

1. Aneka lives in a rural area where access to the Internet is slow and unreliable.

   (a) Explain **two** implications this has for Aneka. [4]

   (b) Give **two** other reasons why some people may not be able to use technology to access services and information. [2]

2. 91% of 16-24 year olds use a mobile phone to go online compared with just 21% of 65-74 year olds. Explain **one** possible reason for this. [2]

3. Paul has poor eyesight.
   Explain **two** 'reasonable adjustments' Paul's employer could make to enable Paul to work effectively. [4]

4. Discuss how the loss of net neutrality could impact on access to services and information. [6]

Chapter 15
Acceptable use policies

Objectives

- Understand the purpose and use of acceptable use policies
- Understand the blurring of social and business boundaries
  - use of social media for business purposes
  - impact of personal use of digital systems on professional life

Acceptable use policies

As covered in Chapter 11, by far the greatest risk to the security of an organisation's digital systems and data are insiders – the employees, contractors and temporary staff who work for the organisation.

It's not enough to simply tell them not to use their work computers for non-work-related activities, to remember to lock their laptop away before they leave the office or never to click on a link in a phishing email.

The purpose of the **acceptable use policy (AUP)** is to spell out unambiguously to everyone working for an organisation what is and is not acceptable behaviour. It lays down a formal set of rules that limit the ways in which network and computer equipment can be used.

Providing it is properly enforced, an AUP will help prevent:

- digital devices and networks being damaged by malware
- criminals getting hold of sensitive data, confidential information or intellectual property
- legal action resulting from breaches of data protection, copyright and other legislation
- employees wasting time and network bandwidth on non-work-related Internet activities

At the start of an AUP there are three short sections – an **overview** giving the purpose of the policy, a **scope** section identifying who the policy applies to and an **assets** section listing the equipment, documents and knowledge that are covered by the policy.

Company Acceptable Use Policy

Overview
The purpose of this policy is to establish acceptable and unacceptable use of information and IT equipment, network resources and mobile IT equipment at the company.

Scope
This policy applies to all Company employees, contractors, temporary employees and agents.

Assets
This policy applies to:
- Computer devices, networks and other digital systems owned or leased by the company.
- All information, in whatever form, relating to the Company business activities and to all information handled by the Company relating to other organisations with which it deals.

Your responsibilities
You are responsible for the security of the information and systems that are under your control.

The next two sections are a lot longer. They spell out what constitutes **acceptable behaviour** – what staff are required to do, and **unacceptable behaviour** – what they are not allowed to do.

Equipment

We expect you to:

- Secure all computing devices with a password protected screensaver, with the automatic feature set to 10 minutes or less.
- Lock the screen or log off when you leave the computing device unattended.
- Place your laptop in a locked drawer or cabinet if leaving it at the company premises overnight.
- Promptly report the theft of company assets to a member of Technical Services.

Passwords

- Keep passwords secure and **DO NOT** share them with anyone. This includes family and other household members when work is being completed at home.

Proprietary information

- Only access, use or share Company proprietary information to the extent it is authorised and necessary to fulfil your assigned job role.
- Promptly report the loss or unauthorised disclosure of Company proprietary information.

Internet and email

Use extreme caution when opening email attachments received from unknown senders, which may contain malware.

You are not permitted to:

Proprietary information

- Store proprietary information belonging to the Company on any personal or non-company device.
- Reveal any confidential or proprietary information to parties outside of the Company.
- Provide information about or lists of Company employees to outside or third parties.

Illegal activity

- Violate copyright law by making unauthorised copies of copyrighted material or installing copyrighted software for which the Company does not have an active licence.
- Engage in any form of illegal activity while using Company owned digital systems.

Network use

- Access data, servers or accounts to which you are not authorised.
- Circumvent user authentication on any device or network account.
- Reveal your network ID and/or password to others or allow someone else to use your login details.
- Intentionally install malicious code on any company digital systems including viruses, worms, Trojan horses, email bombs, spyware, adware and key loggers.

The next section covers **monitoring**. It states how the staff's behaviour will be monitored to check that they are complying with the policy. The **sanctions** that will be applied to anyone found to be breaking the rules are given in the penultimate section.

Monitoring

- In order to ensure compliance with this policy, personnel authorised by the Company will monitor activity on digital systems, including internet and email use.
- We will investigate where reasonable suspicion exists of a breach of this policy.

Sanctions

- An employee found to have violated this policy will be subject to disciplinary action, up to and including termination of employment.
- A violation of this policy by a contractor, consultant, temporary or other worker may result in the termination of their contract with the Company.

Staff must acknowledge that they have read and agree to abide by the policy. The final section lets them register their **agreement** either by signing a paper copy of the document or clicking an 'agree' button in a digital version.

Many organisations provide initial AUP training and follow-up refresher courses for staff to ensure that they are fully aware of what they must and must not do.

A designated senior manager, usually the IT Director, will have overall responsibility for overseeing and updating the AUP.

 What do you think an AUP should say about use of social media?

Blurring of social and business boundaries

Social media are web-based communication channels that enable people to interact with each other by both sharing and consuming information.

Unlike traditional forms of media – newspapers, TV, radio – social media aren't just one-way channels. They interact with people whilst giving them information. This can be done by asking for their comments, letting them vote on something or making personal recommendations for them based on the ratings of other people with similar interests.

Facebook is the biggest social media platform, with more than two billion people using it every month.

Thanks to social media, the boundaries between public and private, business and personal are becoming blurred.

People post information about themselves on social media platforms that not so long ago they would have kept private. Organisations are using the same platforms for business purposes and encouraging people to interact with them on social media.

 Find out which other social media platforms are popular. How do they differ from one another?

Use of social media for business purposes

With nearly half of the world's population using social media, it's not surprising that organisations – large and small – are embracing social media for a variety of business purposes.

- **Engaging with customers.** It is a great way for organisations to engage with their customers, receive feedback on their products and services and respond promptly to questions and complaints.
- **Personalising adverts.** Advertising on a social media platform is an inexpensive way to attract new customers. Adverts can be personalised or target people in a particular group based on factors such as age group, location or interests.
- **Showcasing products.** Organisations can showcase their products and post photographs of customers enjoying them to encourage others to do the same.
- **Driving traffic to their website.** Organisations can use social media posts to drive traffic to their website and increase their search engine rankings.
- **Building brand awareness.** Getting people with a large following on social media talking about them and their products favourably is a good way for organisations to build brand awareness and increase sales.
- **Gathering market intelligence.** Organisations can tap into social media to find out what people are saying about them and their competitors.
- **Filling job vacancies.** Professional networking sites, such as LinkedIn, can help organisations attract skilled employees.

Case study: 15-year old Eddie becomes the likeable face of Southern Rail

In July 2017, a Year 11 pupil called Eddie was on work experience at Southern Rail. The rail company had been in trouble for months over constant delays, cancelled trains and action by drivers. But all that was forgotten when Eddie was allowed to take over the company's Twitter feed. The account's 100,000 plus followers, who usually bombarded the feed with angry tweets, loved Eddie. All of a sudden no-one was complaining about late-running trains any more!

Q3
The American fast food chain Wendy's uses social media very effectively to promote and grow the business. Find out how.

Impact of personal use of digital systems on professional life

According to one recent survey, people spend on average nearly 2.5 hours per day on social networking and messaging platforms.

Most organisations allow employees to use social media, with certain provisos.

- It mustn't interfere with their work.
- They mustn't reveal confidential information.
- They mustn't post anything that might damage the reputation of their employer.
- They mustn't make disparaging, defamatory or harassing comments or say anything derogatory about competitors.
- They must add a disclaimer to any posts stating that the opinions they express are strictly their own and not those of their employer.

For some employees, being active on social media is part of their job. People who work in sales, marketing, customer service and public relations spend much of their working life online.

Image and reputation

An individual's profile on social media says a great deal about them. The digital footprints they leave behind may show them in a bad light. Foolish comments or unflattering images from the past could affect their chance of landing their 'dream' job.

Most employers research prospective candidates on social media before interviewing them and make some decisions based on the information they find there.

Many people wanting to improve their job prospects or land new contracts build up their reputation online and use social media to showcase their achievements.

The **Data Protection Act 2018** gives individuals the 'right to be forgotten' – to request that personal content about them is permanently removed from social media. You can read more about this in Chapter 16.

Q4
Some employers take a dim view of employees who post too frequently.
Why do you think this is the case?

Networking

There are a number of social networks for professionals – people in work and those seeking work.

Joining a professional community, such as Linkedin, allows members to:

- connect with other professionals in their field
- post their CV online for potential employers to see
- find out about other companies and gain useful insights
- search for jobs
- join specialist groups and get support from other, more experienced, members
- publish blog posts to a large audience
- take part in online workshops to enhance their skillset
- be recommended by other members

Exercises

1. Nils is the IT Director at Red Top Limited. He has produced an acceptable use policy for the company.

    (a) Give **three** reasons why the company should have an acceptable use policy,   [3]

    (b) All employees are required to sign the acceptable use policy.

    Explain why this is the case.   [2]

2. Layla is a graphic designer.

    Describe **two** ways in which she can use social media for work-related purposes.   [4]

3. Gareth works in the sales department of a company. He frequently posts on social media.

    Gareth is considering joining an online professional community.

    (a) Explain **two** advantages to Gareth of joining an online community.   [4]

    (b) Gareth is applying for jobs in other companies.

    Discuss how his use of social media may influence prospective employers.

Chapter 16
Data Protection

Objectives

- Understand data protection principles
- Understand the use of data on the Internet:
    - right to be forgotten
    - appropriate and legal use of cookies and other transactional data
- To develop understanding of intellectual property

Data protection principles

Organisations collect and store huge quantities of personal data. Employee records, loyalty schemes, sales transactions and customer accounts all contain sensitive information.

The **Data Protection Act 2018** is the UK's implementation of the General Data Protection Regulation (GDPR), which is designed to protect individuals against misuse of their personal data. It contains a set of principles that organisations must adhere to.

Data protection principle	What this means for organisations
Lawfulness, fairness and transparency	They must have a legitimate reason for processing a person's data and must not use it for any other purpose. They must tell the person what they'll use their data for and get their consent.
Purpose limitation	They must only use the data for the specific purpose for which it was collected. For example, a supermarket that collects transactional data about a customer's purchases, can't use that data for marketing purposes without first getting the customer's consent.
Data minimisation	They must only obtain as much data about a person as is necessary for the specified purpose. For example, a seed company that wants to send out a catalogue to its customers, only needs their name and address. They don't need their date of birth or email address.
Accuracy	They must ensure that the data they collect is accurate and up-to-date. When notified of an error in the data, they must update it promptly.
Storage limitation	They must not keep data for any longer than is necessary.
Security	They must keep data secure and protect it against unauthorised or unlawful processing, accidental loss, destruction or damage.
Accountability	Organisations must be able to demonstrate that their data protection measures are sufficient .
Transfer	Data cannot be transferred to other countries with less protection.

Data subjects' rights

Under the Data Protection Act 2018, individuals have the right to find out what information the government and other organisations store about you. These include the right to:

- be informed about how their data is being used
- access personal data
- have incorrect data updated
- have data erased
- stop or restrict the processing of their data
- data portability (to get and reuse personal data for their own purposes across different services)
- object to how their data is processed in certain circumstances

Obligations of organisations

The Act requires organisations holding personal data:

- to register with the Information Commissioner's Office (ICO)
- to carry out a data protection impact assessment to identify, assess and minimise privacy risks
- to appoint a Data Protection Officer with responsibility for ensuring that appropriate measures are taken to collect, hold and use data in accordance with the law
- to notify affected individuals and the ICO if a data breach occurs
- not to transfer data to regions not bound by similar data protection principles

The ICO has the authority to fine organisations for non-compliance. In 2018 it fined Facebook £500,000 – the maximum amount under the law at that time – for allowing Cambridge Analytica to use personal data from Facebook users for political purposes without the users' permission.

Data and the use of the Internet

As you saw in Chapter 12, a huge volume of personal data is being produced every day. It is the role of governments to protect it and define what can and cannot be done with it.

The right to be forgotten

The Data Protection Act gives individuals the right to be forgotten – to have personal data about themselves deleted.

Individuals can request that personal data about them is deleted. This includes files, records in a database, backup copies and any copies that may have been moved into an archive. It enables individuals to ask social media companies to delete posts that they published earlier in their lives and search engines to remove material about them from online searches.

Case study: Google's response to the right to be forgotten

The European Union Court of Justice (ECJ) ruled in 2014 that individuals living in one of the 27 countries of the EU have a right to require Google to remove sensitive information about them from its search results.

Since then, there has been an ongoing battle in the courts to determine if Google also has to censor results in the US and elsewhere. The ECJ may come down in favour of Google, meaning that anyone using google.com rather than google.co.uk will still be able to see the censored information.

Legal use of cookies and other transactional data

The **Privacy and Electronic Communications Regulations (PECR) 2003** govern the use of cookies and other forms of transactional data.

If a website uses cookies, it must display a message telling users that this is the case and get their consent. Users have the right to opt out of having data about them collected in this way. The website must also publish a privacy policy explaining what data it collects and how it is used. You can find out more about cookies in Chapter 12.

The same rules apply to similar technologies and other types of technology, including apps on mobile phones, tablets, smart TVs or other digital devices. They also ban spyware and other covert surveillance software that downloads to a user's device and tracks their activities without their knowledge.

The PECR also requires Internet service providers and telecoms providers to keep personal data secure when it is being stored or transmitted.

Intellectual property

Intellectual property (IP) is defined as creations of the mind, such as inventions, literary works, designs, logos or a smartphone app. IP is a valuable asset that gives companies a competitive edge, accounting – according to one estimate – for around 80% of the average company's value. Needless to say, a company is bound to suffer financially if its original IP is used by someone else without permission.

Methods of identifying and protecting IP

Trademarks, copyright and patents all provide protection for IP.

A **trademark** is a badge of ownership. The ™ symbol denotes a trademark that hasn't been officially registered. The ® symbol denotes a registered trademark.

Logos, wording, sounds, colours and shapes can all be registered as trademarks, providing they are unique. The owner of a trademark has exclusive use of it. Organisations use trademarks to distinguish their goods and services from those of their competitors. Trademarks identify IP but do not protect it.

Copyright is granted to the creator of an original work, such as a book, a film, or a piece of music. It grants them the legal right to control all use of the work. Copyright doesn't protect the idea of a work, only how it is expressed.

The © symbol indicates that a product or work is protected by copyright. Copyright remains in place until 70 years after the death of the registered holder.

A **patent** offers different protection than copyright. It protects inventions. It is an exclusive right granted to an inventor to make, use and sell an invention for a fixed period of time – usually 20 years. In order to get a patent, the creator has to be able to demonstrate that what they have invented is distinct from anything else that already exists.

> ## Case study: Patent wars
>
> It took seven years for the patent war fought between Apple and Samsung to end. The two companies have been battling in the courts over patent infringements relating to key components of their mobile phones since 2011. They finally agreed to call the battle off and reached an out-of-court settlement in July 2018. The dispute illustrates just how valuable patents are.

Legal and ethical use of IP

The **Copyright, Designs and Patents Act 1988** makes it a criminal offence to copy, modify or distribute intellectual property without permission.

Only the person who holds the copyright for an original work has the right to reproduce, distribute and adapt it. They can however issue a **licence** giving someone else **permission** to use copyrighted material, subject to certain terms and conditions, e.g. for how long and for what purposes the licensee (the holder of the licence) is allowed to use the work.

Some copyright holders release their work under a **creative commons licence**. There are a number of creative commons licences for them to choose from, some more restrictive than others.

The most accommodating one is **attribution**. This allows others to distribute, remix, tweak, and build upon an original work, even commercially, as long as they credit the copyright owner for the original creation.

> **Q2** How many creative commons licence types are there? Which is the most restrictive?

Downloading music, movies or sport content for free from a peer-to-peer file sharing site or streaming them from a dubious website is illegal and constitutes copyright infringement.

The Federation Against Copyright Theft (FACT) represents the interests of copyright owners, cinema owners and legal streaming services such as Spotify in the UK. According to FACT, the UK's creative industries lose around £500 million a year due to breach of copyright.

When questioned about their media consumption, many people say that choice is far more important to them than legal or ethical considerations – even price is less important than availability. Copyright infringement is illegal. It is also unethical, since it deprives the creators of the works of being paid for what they have produced. In the long term, they may not have the money to continue creating new content or may not think it is worth their while.

Exercises

1. An online music streaming service collects data about its customers. This enables it to recommend relevant albums to them.

    (a) Explain **one** way in which legislation protects customers from misuse of this data.   [2]

    (b) Explain **two** ways in which streaming sports content from an illegal website will impact on the content creators.   [4]

2. Werner is a freelance film producer. He registers the copyright to every film he makes.

    Explain why content owners copyright their content.   [3]

3. Complete the table, with **one** tick in each row.   [5]

Description	Intellectual property	Patent	Licence	Copyright	Trade mark
Permission given by the owner of a work to another person					
Works that are the product of original creative thought					
Grant of protection for an invention, lasting 20 years					
Legal protection for the creator of a work					
A unique symbol indicating that a product is produced by a particular company					

4. Intellectual property rights are critical to the survival of a business.

    Explain how a business can use each of the following to protect its intellectual property.

    (a) Trademarks   [2]

    (b) Copyright   [2]

    (c) Patents   [2]

Chapter 17
Criminal use of computer systems

Objectives

- To understand the criminal use of computer systems including:
  - ○ Unauthorised access and modification of materials
  - ○ Creation and spreading of malware

Cybercrime

A **cybercriminal** is a person who uses a computer to carry out criminal activity.

Crime statistics

Based on its 2018 crime survey results, the Office for National Statistics (ONS) estimates that around 1.2 million computer misuse crimes were committed against individuals in England and Wales in 2018 – 31% fewer than in the previous year. The fall was mainly due to a reduction in reported incidents of malware – a consequence of better anti-malware software being installed on home networks and personal digital devices.

The ONS estimates that there were 528,000 incidents involving unauthorised access to personal information – including hacking. About the same as in the previous year.

Figures for cybercrime directed at organisations are collected separately by the Department for Digital, Culture, Media & Sport. Its 2019 Cyber Security Breaches Survey indicates that 32% of businesses and 22% of charities were the victims of some kind of cybercrime during the course of the previous 12 months – 14% fewer than in 2018.

 Q1 Suggest a reason for the fall in the number of victims of cybercrime from 2018 to 2019.

Computer Misuse

The **Computer Misuse Act 1990** is the legislation that is used to prosecute cybercriminals in the UK. Offences charged under the act include hacking, unauthorised encryption of data as part of a ransomware attack, dissemination of malware and data theft. In order to keep abreast of the ever-changing nature of cybercrime, the Act has been updated several times since it was first passed by Parliament in 1990.

The Act has four sections, each dealing with a different form of computer misuse.

Unauthorised access to computer material (Section 1). For example, the following are guilty of this offence:

- A husband who tries out multiple passwords until he hits upon the right one to access his wife's email account.
- An employee who looks at sensitive information stored on a company server that they do not have permission to access.

An individual can only be convicted of this offence if it can be shown that they acted with intent. Accessing data by accident is not a crime.

Someone convicted of this offence faces a prison sentence of up to two years, a fine or both.

Case study: Bank manager guilty of unauthorised access

In 2018, a bank manager who worked for Santander pleaded guilty to an offence under Section 1 of the Computer Misuse Act. Her boyfriend talked her into giving him sensitive customer information, which he used to make £15,000 worth of fraudulent transactions. Staff at the bank got suspicious when her staff ID was linked to a number of customer accounts which suffered fraud.

She received a 12-month community order for 160 hours of unpaid work and was fined £300. Needless to say, she lost her job at the bank.

Unauthorised access with intent to commit or facilitate further offences (Section 2). A hacker who uses spyware to harvest credit card details in order to steal money from people's bank accounts is guilty of this offence. It carries a prison sentence of up to five years or a fine, or both.

Unauthorised acts with intent to impair the operation of a computer (Section 3). Someone who distributes malware that deletes or corrupts data stored on a computer is guilty of this offence. As is a hacker who starts a ransomware attack that encrypts data stored on a company server, making it unreadable. The penalty is a prison sentence of up to ten years, a fine or both.

If the damage puts human life or national security in danger, the offender could be sentenced to life imprisonment.

Case study: Teenager gains access to US intelligence data

In 2017, a Leicestershire teenager pleaded guilty to eight offences under Section 1 and two under Section 3 of the Computer Misuse Act and was sentenced to two years in prison.

From his bedroom in Leicestershire, the 15-year-old used social engineering tactics to access plans for intelligence operations in Afghanistan and Iran by pretending to be John Brennan, Director of the CIA, and James Clapper, US Director of National Intelligence. Amongst other illegal activities, he took control of James Clapper's telecoms account, accessed his private emails and redirected his incoming calls.

He was finally caught in February 2016 after gaining unauthorised access to details of 20,000 FBI employees stored on the US Department of Justice's network.

Making, supplying or obtaining articles for use in computer misuse offences (Section 4). Someone who creates and sells toolkits for launching denial of service or malware attacks is guilty of this offence. The penalty is a prison sentence of up to two years, a fine or both.

 Q2 In 2017, mobile phone maker Apple was forced to apologise for having reduced the speed of the iPhone 6 without telling anyone. Some people consider that Apple's action contravened Section 3 of the Computer Misuse Act. What do you think?

The Computer Misuse Act applies if the individual who commits unauthorised access or the target computer/system is located in the UK.

Prosecutions

It seems that cybercriminals often get away with their crimes. In 2017 there were just 47 prosecutions for computer misuse. The police concede that they don't have sufficient resources or expertise to investigate every incident properly. Many crimes are carried out by people based outside the UK, which makes it harder to prosecute them.

Exercises

1. Complete the table to identify the legislation that applies in each situation.   [5]

Situation	DPA	PECR	CMA	DEA	CDPA
The inhabitants of a small village in the country rarely get broadband download speeds of above 8 Mbps.					
A motorbike spares company passes its customer mailing list on to a safety equipment supplier without first asking customers.					
A student streams a pirated copy of a movie she wants to watch from an online site.					
A website uses persistent cookies to give customers a personalised experience but fails to tell them that it does so.					
An employee uses his manager's ID and password to find out how much other people in her department earn.					

DPA: The Data Protection Act
CMA: Computer Misuse Act
CDPA: Copyright, Designs and Patents Act

PECR: Privacy and Electronic Communications Regulations
DEA: Digital Economy Act

2. A teenager sells virus kits on the Internet that enable other people to create and spread malware.
    State which offence under the Computer Misuse Act they are is guilty of.   [1]

3. Cybercrime causes significant harm to individuals, organisations and society.
    Discuss how the Computer Misuse Act helps to deter cybercriminals.   [6]

Planning and communication in digital systems

In this section:

Chapter 18
Data and information flow diagrams

Objectives

- Understand how organisations use information and data flow diagrams to explain systems, data and information

- Be able to interpret information presented in the form of a data flow diagram or an information flow diagram

- Draw a data flow diagram or an information flow diagram representing a given scenario

Presenting information

Information may be presented in a number of different ways, for example:

- A written description

- A table

- A chart or graph

- A diagram

What would be the best way of presenting the following information?

Q1

(a) The average daily maximum temperature in a particular town over a one-year period

(b) Instructions on how to assemble a piece of flat-pack furniture

(c) A holiday itinerary

(d) A procedure for validating a password

(e) How data flows between a team of people collaborating on a project, using cloud storage

Data flow diagram

A data flow diagram shows what information will be input to a business information system, how it gets to the next stage in the processing, who inputs it and who receives it. It may also show how and where it is stored. It is used to show, in a graphical way, an overview of a computer system, without going into any detail.

There are certain standard symbols that are commonly used in data flow diagrams.

Process or event. A **process** could be, for example, 'place an order', 'look up information in a database' or 'calculate total invoice value'.

Input/Output or external entity inputting or receiving information. An **external entity** may be, for example, a person or a department

File / Database

Data or information flow

Alternative sets of symbols are sometimes used; for example, an oval for an external entity and a rectangle for a process or function. So long as you are consistent and label all entities, processes, data stores and data flows, the symbols or shapes you use are not important.

Example 1

Dave is a traffic policeman who patrols the roads. His car has a licence plate reader which scans the licence plate of every car that is parked or moving as he drives by. Information about any car which has a lapsed registration or insurance, is stolen or has an owner who is wanted by the police will automatically be displayed on his screen. The information includes the year, make and model of the car, who it is registered to, and whether the registration is current, as well as the address of whoever it is registered to.

Here is a labelled data flow diagram (DFD) representing this system.

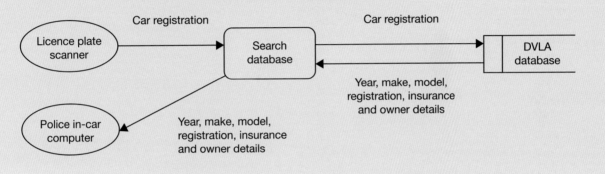

Example 2

A registered customer logs in to an online shopping site. The computer system checks their ID and password on a customer file. A message is displayed on the customer's screen if the ID is invalid.

Otherwise, no message is displayed. (The order is then taken, but this is not shown on the diagram.)

Here is a labelled data flow diagram to describe this process.

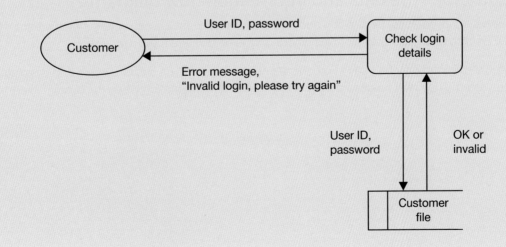

Information flow diagram

An information flow diagram (IFD) is similar to a data flow diagram (DFD), but shows only the exchange of information between individuals or departments.

Example 3

A school supplier accepts orders entered by a customer by phone, fax, email or mail. The clerk in the Sales and Invoicing department records the order on the computer system.

The information flow diagram shown below shows how information flows between the customer and the various departments which handle the order.

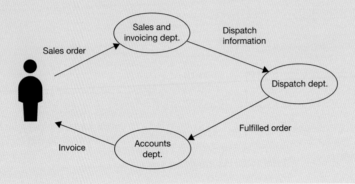

 Q2 Describe in words how the ordering system works. What assumptions have been made in this information flow diagram?

It does not matter if you show a simple box instead of an icon for the customer, or draw a straight line instead of a squiggly one. As long as the meaning is clear and the departments and information flows are shown, there is no one "correct" way of drawing the diagram.

How organisations use data and information flow diagrams

IFDs show information as sources, destination and flows. DFDs show processes where inputs are transformed into outputs. DFDs also show databases or files where data is held within the systems.

Both these types of diagram may be used in organisations to explain how a system works and what data or information is involved. They may be used during design, or as documentation when the system is up and running.

Exercises

1. Susan is writing an essay on Ancient Egypt. She searches for "Ancient Egypt" and finds a useful website.

   (a) She copies references to the information, images and website address from the site to a document saved on her hard disk with a file name "Useful resources". She uses some of the information from this file to inform her essay.

   Draw an information flow diagram to represent this process.   [4]

   (b) Give **two** reasons why she may have saved the address of the website.   [2]

2. Fred queues at the cinema to buy tickets for a film. The assistant checks availability on his computer terminal and prints the required number of tickets. Fred pays by cash and receives the tickets.

   Copy and label the data flow diagram to show the data flow in this system.   [6]

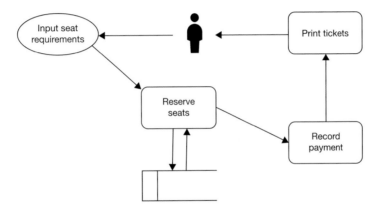

3. CompuTrain is an organisation providing remote, online IT training courses.

   At the end of each course, registered students sit an online multiple-choice exam.

   (a) A data flow diagram representing this system is shown below.

   Use the diagram to explain how this system works.   [6]

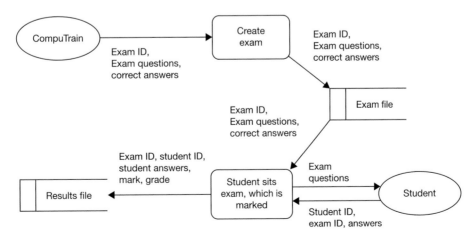

   (b) Students can log on to find out their mark and grade.

   Draw a data flow diagram to represent this part of the system.   [4]

Chapter 19
Flowcharts

Objectives

- Understand how organisations use flowcharts
- Be able to interpret a flowchart in a range of contexts
- Use flowchart symbols to represent the steps of an activity

What is an algorithm?

An **algorithm** is a sequence of steps specifying how to perform a task or solve a problem. It could be a set of instructions on how to assemble a bookcase, a recipe for making a cake, or instructions on how to calculate the discount on an item costing £125.

Using a flowchart to represent an activity or algorithm

A flowchart is a graphical way of representing a series of steps.

Drawing a flowchart is one method a systems analyst may use to show the individual steps in a process. Or, a flowchart could be used to show how a policy or procedure should be followed; for example, the steps in a disaster recovery procedure.

A programmer may use a flowchart to work out exactly how to solve a problem. Once a flowchart has been drawn, the programmer can write the program code corresponding to the flowchart.

Standard symbols are used to show the input, processing and output comprising the system. Arrows should be drawn where necessary to show the direction of flow. By default, the direction of flow is from top to bottom, START to END, of the flowchart.

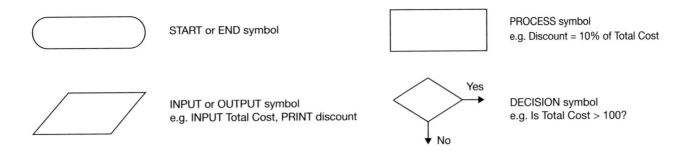

START or END symbol

PROCESS symbol
e.g. Discount = 10% of Total Cost

INPUT or OUTPUT symbol
e.g. INPUT Total Cost, PRINT discount

DECISION symbol
e.g. Is Total Cost > 100?

Example 1

An online store charges postage and packing of £5.00 on all orders with a value of less than £20. If the total order value is greater than or equal to £20, postage and packing is free. The order value and Postage and Packing (PP) charge is printed. Here is a flowchart showing the input, processing and output.

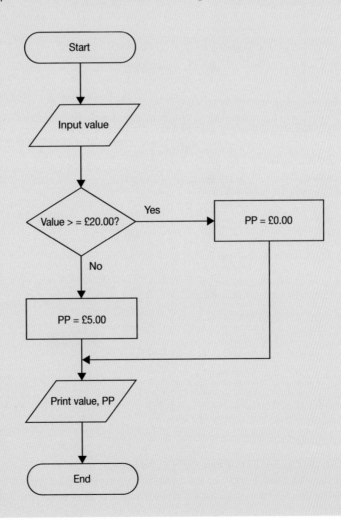

 Q1 Amend the flowchart shown in Example 1 so that the process of calculating order values and Postage and Packing continues until a whole batch of orders has been processed.

Flowcharting a loop

Some algorithms involve performing the same sequence of steps many times, until some condition is true. Some processes loop endlessly until the computer is switched off.

Example 2

Draw a flowchart representing the process of returning a book to a library.

In the flowchart below, the user chooses the option "Quick return" which does not require a library card to be scanned.

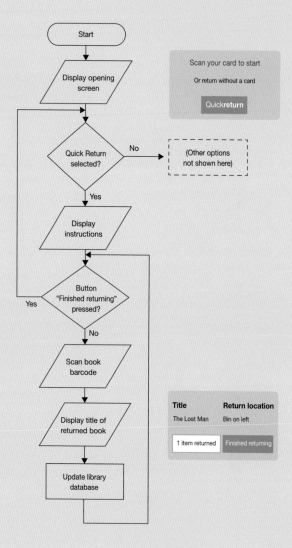

 Q2 Users can generally be relied upon to do something unexpected. What will happen if the user tries to return the same book twice? How could the flowchart be amended to cope with this situation?

Does the flowchart allow for a user who presses the "Finished returning" button without scanning any book barcodes?

What other options would be displayed if the user presents their card to be scanned to start instead of pressing "Quick return"?

Exercises

1. Ana has a smartphone which she uses for phone calls, texts, emails, browsing the Internet and downloading music. Her standard monthly tariff is £45, which includes a monthly data allowance of 4GB. If she exceeds her data allowance, she pays an extra charge depending on how much extra data she uses.

   (a) Complete the following flowchart elements A, B, C and D to calculate the amount she pays each month. [4]

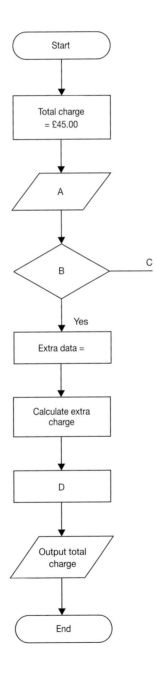

   (b) The extra charge is £6 for every 250MB of data used. Calculate the total charge if Ana uses an extra 0.75GB of data in one month. (1GB = 1000MB) [2]

2. Each employee in AB Services Ltd has a unique ID to log in to the company network. Employees can choose their own ID when they first register on the system.

   The computer asks the new user to enter an ID. It checks the ID entered with those already stored in the system. If the ID is already in use, a message "Choose another ID" is displayed, otherwise the new ID is saved. This process is repeated until a valid ID is entered.

   Draw a flowchart to represent this procedure.   [6]

3. Kiara works for a software company which creates and sells computer games. She is devising a game for young children.

   A moving balloon appears on the screen, and she must pop the balloon by clicking on it with the mouse. When the balloon is popped another one appears. The aim of the game is to pop as many balloons as possible in one minute.

   An incomplete flowchart for the game is shown below.

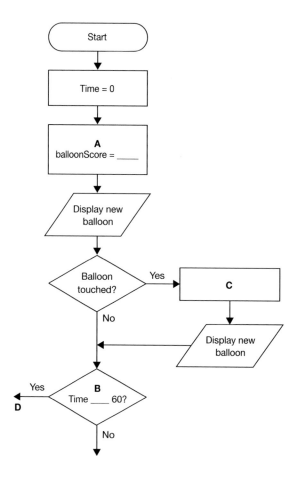

(a) Complete the statement at A.   [1]

(b) Complete the statement at B.   [1]

(c) Complete the statement at C.   [1]

(d) Complete connector D.   [1]

(e) Add a flowchart box at the bottom of the flowchart to display the player's score. [1]

4. Susan sells handmade cards via her online shop. She offers customers two types of postage, 1st class which arrives the next day and 2nd class which arrives in 2–3 days. A flowchart representing this is shown below.

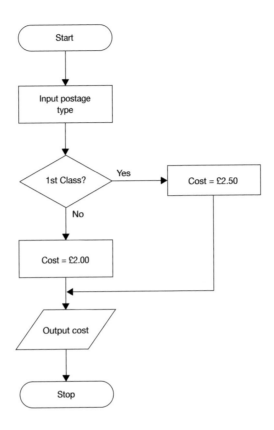

(a) If a customer selects 1st class postage, state the cost that will be output.   [1]

   If a customer orders two or more items the postage doubles in price.

(b) Draw a new flowchart that takes into account the doubling of the price.   [4]

Chapter 20
System diagrams

Objectives

- Understand how organisations use systems diagrams to explain systems
- Be able to interpret a systems diagram in a range of contexts

System diagrams

A computer system consists of hardware and software. The hardware consists of several connected components. A standalone desktop computer, for example, consists of input, output and storage devices. It may be connected to external devices such as a printer, scanner and router.

A system diagram may show how the components of a computer system are connected together. The individual parts of the system may be represented simply by boxes, or sometimes by icons. The direction in which data flows is indicated with arrows.

At its simplest, a system consists of **input**, **processing** and **output**.

Example 1

Janine has a desktop computer. It is connected to a printer and a router, through which she can access the Internet.

Here is a diagram which represents this system.

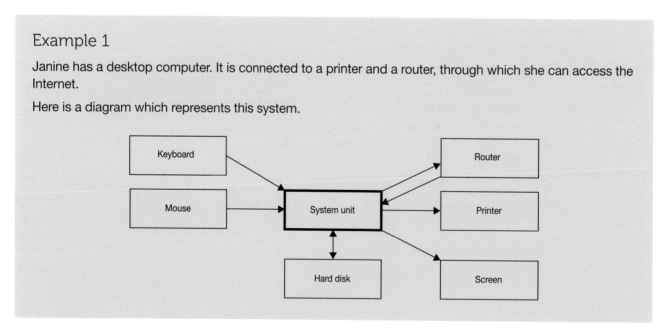

Interpreting a system diagram

The diagram in Example 1 shows only the hardware. The direction of the arrows shows in which direction data will flow, and as this is a standalone PC it is multi-purpose and no further detail needs to be given.

System diagrams used in organisations may typically include the people or departments involved, input devices and data that is input, the processes or events that occur in the system, and the output. This may be, for example, a printed report, a screen display or a signal which causes a window to open or close.

Why organisations use system diagrams

- Diagrams can **display a lot of information** in a small space. They can show all the components, input and output data or signals. They represent multiple connections between components, and show feedback loops in a manner that can be easily grasped and interpreted. "A picture's worth a thousand words", as the saying goes.

- System diagrams are an **excellent way to communicate designs** and information about systems to others.

- They are a design aid, helping the designer to create a workable system before it is implemented. They act as a means of **recording the development of a design**. They can easily be amended as the design evolves.

Example 2

The system diagram below shows a computer system used to maintain ideal growing conditions in a commercial greenhouse.

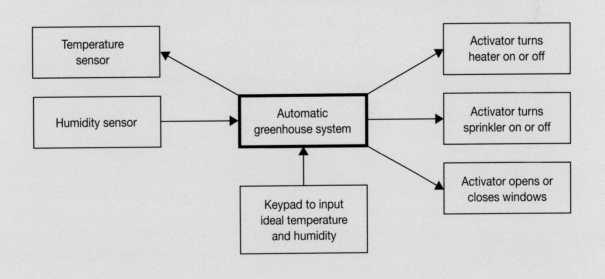

 Q1   **Write a description of the system shown in the system diagram.**

Example 3

Oyster smartcards (using an RFID chip) are used by Transport for London. A person using the London Underground can use their card to touch in at the start of a journey to open the entry barrier. The card reader reads information from the card and calculates whether to allow travel. At the end of the journey, the traveller touches out to complete the transaction. The system assesses and deducts the value of the fare payable and writes back information to the card. If the user fails to touch out, the maximum daily fare is charged.

All transactions are settled between the card and reader alone. Readers transmit the transactions to the main computer system in batches, not in real time. The system keeps a record of transactions that have been completed between cards and readers.

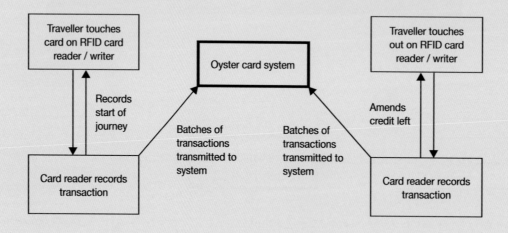

Q2 Write an explanation of how the system could deal with the situation when a traveller fails to 'touch out' at the end of their journey.

Exercises

1. A public library has registered users who have been issued with a library card displaying a bar code which holds the unique user ID.

   Library users use one of the terminals to borrow or return a book.

   (a) Interpret the system diagram shown below to explain how the borrowing system works. [4]

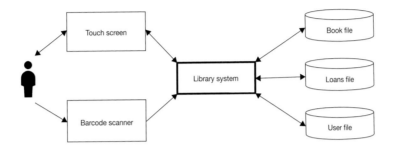

   (b) State **three** items of data that would be held on the Loans file. [3]

   (c) State **two** ways in which the library may use systems diagrams. [2]

2. The system diagram below shows the input, output and data store used in a supermarket system.

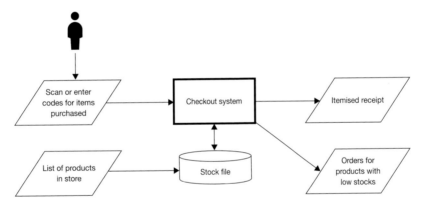

   (a) Describe **two** data processing events in the checkout system that will take place when a customer at the checkout scans an item they have purchased. [4]

   (b) Stock ID, description and quantity in stock are held on the Stock file.

   State **two** other items of information that need to be held on the stock file in order to be able to produce orders for products which have low stocks. [2]

Chapter 21
Tables and written information

Objectives

- Understand how organisations use tables and written information to explain systems and data
- Be able to interpret information presented in tables

Presenting information in tabular form

Organisations of all descriptions collect data from their everyday activities. Monthly sales, exam results, hospital admissions, population and thousands of other tabulated data may be found in company reports or in survey data on the Internet.

Tables are an effective way of presenting information in some cases, such as:

- when you want to show how a particular type of information such as monthly or annual sales figures, temperature or unemployment rate varies over a period of time or in different geographical areas.
- when the dataset contains relatively few numbers. It is hard to take in and interpret long columns of numbers. For example, if a company produces 300 different products, a table showing monthly sales of each product would not be a useful way of presenting information.
- when it is important to show a precise value, e.g. 78.76 rather than 78.72, which may not be obvious in a graph.

How the data is presented in the table makes a difference to how easy it is to take in the information given.

In the table shown below, data has been extracted from population data about all the countries in Europe. The data has been rearranged to show an example of a poorly laid out table.

	Population per square km
France	104
Germany	233
Gibralter (UK)	4328
Greece	81
Iceland	3
Italy	192
Kingdom of the Netherlands	393
Russia	8
Sweden	20
UK	267

Is anything missing? Could it be better laid out? Is the UK one of the most heavily populated countries shown? Suggest some improvements that could be made to this table to improve it and make it easier to extract meaningful information.

The first table has the following faults or weaknesses:

- It has no title.
- The source of the data is not given.
- One of the row titles goes across two lines.
- The lines separating each cell make it harder, rather than easier, to read.
- The figures in the second column should be under the heading.
- The information about the relative population density in different countries would be much easier to grasp if it was arranged in descending numerical order, rather in alphabetical order of countries.

Here is an improved version:

Table 1: Selected European countries by population density

Country	Population per square km
Gibralter (UK)	4328
Netherlands	393
UK	267
Germany	233
Italy	192
France	104
Greece	81
Sweden	20
Russia	8
Iceland	3

Source: https://www.worldatlas.com/articles/european-countries-by-population-density.html

Which countries in this list are more densely populated than the UK? Does Germany have a higher population density than the Netherlands?

Interpreting information in a table

The way that a table is designed has a big impact on how easily the information can be interpreted.

- Consider how a table is best laid out between rows and columns. The table below shows the sales over three years of each of four products sold by a training shoe manufacturer.

Shoe sales in £ 2016–2018			
	Lifestyle	Running	Training	Tennis
2016	38,547.43	26,690.00	17,236.65	12,886.75
2017	35,844.50	32,115.99	15,477.42	15,871.50
2018	33,659.79	35,271.70	12,863.98	18,852.50

It is generally easier to identify patterns when reading down a column rather than across a row. If the purpose is to highlight which product has the highest turnover each year, the table should be planned so that the data is shown in the columns, not the rows.

- Figures should not be shown to a level of accuracy which does not add anything to the general picture. There is no need to show the pence in this table.

	Product sales in £ 2016–2018		
	2016	**2017**	**2018**
Lifestyle	38,547	35,845	33,660
Running	26,690	32,116	35,272
Training	17,237	15,477	12,864
Tennis	12,887	15,872	18,853

- The table should be given an explicit title that needs no further explanation.
- Shading and bold text helps to make headings stand out.

Using graphs

Data such as that above has been entered into a spreadsheet and can very easily be turned into a graph. A bar chart could show how each product is performing over the three-year period.

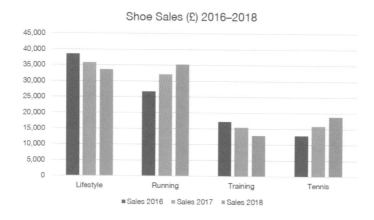

A pie chart will show what proportion of turnover each product contributes to the overall sales in a particular year.

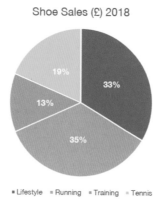

 Compare the table and the two charts shown above in terms of completeness, amount of detail, and presentation. Which type of shoe has shown the biggest increase in sales? Which type of shoe contributed most to total sales in 2016? In 2018?

Written information

When information is presented in the form of a chart or graph, further explanation and an analysis of the data is often helpful. Why are sales of shoes rising? Is this the result of hiring an expert on sports shoe construction, or participating in an annual exhibition, or building a new advertising campaign?

The chart below shows the approximate television viewing figures in the UK in 2017.

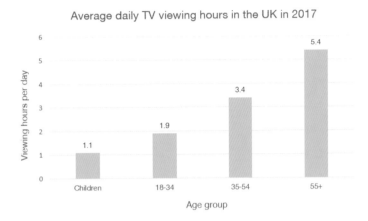

Average daily TV viewing hours in the UK in 2017

Here is an analysis of TV viewing figures from a different survey:

"Television remains the most used electronic medium for UK children and adults. On average, UK citizens aged 18 and older spend over three hours a day watching TV. This is in addition to the average two hours and 35 minutes they interact with their smartphone on an average day.

Television is still a highly valued media format but there is a decline in the use of television amongst younger viewers that is not encouraging for TV networks in the long run. The older generation (55+) may include retirees who arguably have considerably more time available for television, but the growing use of newer media formats such as YouTube and Netflix, particularly amongst the younger generations, shows a trend moving away from 'traditional' television viewing.

The younger generation are spending considerably less time watching broadcast television than five years ago, but do spend time watching alternative entertainment on their television sets. Broadcasters need to confront the challenges posed by online streaming companies to ensure that they can continue to produce high-quality shows that appeal to all generations."

Q2

Read the above explanation of the survey findings and answer the questions:

(a) Do UK adults on average spend more time on their smartphones than watching TV? If so, by approximately how much time?

(b) Why does the report suggest that the trend "is not encouraging for TV networks in the long run"?

Impact of information on decision making

Information is used by senior managers in organisations to help with decision-making. In a manufacturing company, for example, it is important to know how sales have been trending over the past few years. If sales of some products are going down while others are increasing, what is the reason and what should be done about it? Having accurate, up-to-date information clearly presented will help managers to spot problem areas and make appropriate decisions.

The quality of information is measured in terms of:

- source/collection method
- accuracy
- age
- completeness
- amount of detail
- format/presentation
- volume

System documentation

When a new system is purchased, for example an accounts package for a small business, it normally comes with written documentation, either in printed form or online.

There may be a user manual going through each menu option in a package, or an online help system which lets the user specify what they need help with:

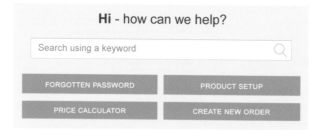

If the user types in, for example 'new order', they may see a screen something like this:

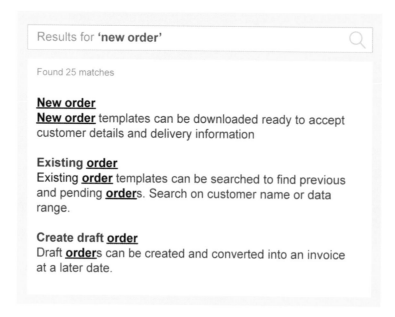

Exercises

1. For each of the following, explain whether you would use written information, a table or a bar chart to present the following information:

    (a) Average broadband speeds in the ten countries with the fastest broadband. [2]

    (b) Exam results for a class of 25 students. [2]

    (c) The route between Birmingham and Calais giving times and distances for each leg of the journey. [2]

2. The charts below show numbers of rentals and average prices of accommodation in people's spare rooms in cities around the world for people visiting cities for a few days.

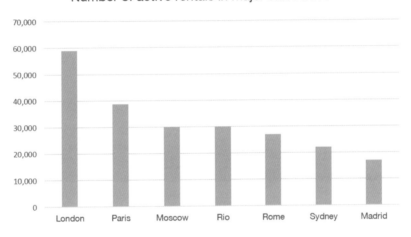

Number of active rentals in major cities 2018

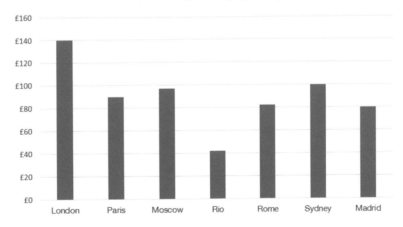

Average charge per night

Discuss the information shown in the charts. [6]

3. The table and chart below show the average readership of a national daily newspaper over a period of five years. Two half-yearly periods are shown for each year.

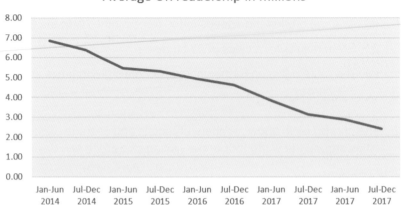

Average UK readership in millions

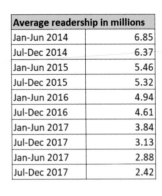

Average readership in millions	
Jan-Jun 2014	6.85
Jul-Dec 2014	6.37
Jan-Jun 2015	5.46
Jul-Dec 2015	5.32
Jan-Jun 2016	4.94
Jul-Dec 2016	4.61
Jan-Jun 2017	3.84
Jul-Dec 2017	3.13
Jan-Jun 2017	2.88
Jul-Dec 2017	2.42

(a) Explain **one** reason the average readership is not the same as number of copies printed.   [2]

(b) Explain the meaning of the value 3.13 as at Jul–Dec 2017 in the table.   [2]

(c) Describe the information that this table and accompanying graph shows.   [2]

(d) Give **two** possible reasons for the trend shown by the graph.   [2]

(e) Information may be presented in **reports**, **tables** or **charts**.

   In the context of the example given regarding average newspaper readership, discuss the advantages and disadvantages of each of these three methods of presentation.   [6]

Index

BTEC L1/2 DIT Teaching Units

Exclusively for teachers

To accompany each section in the textbook, there is a series of teaching units for the new Pearson BTEC Level 1/2 Tech Award in Digital Information Technology.

Each unit contains editable PPT and DOC format materials to enable effective delivery of the content with relevant and engaging examples for students.

There are worksheets and homework for each topic and an assessment test at the end of each unit with exam style questions.

Answers to all worksheets, homework tasks and the assessment are also included.

Unit D is free to registered teachers.

Downloadable Units to support the Pearson BTEC Tech Award DIT Specification:

Pack A: Modern technologies
Pack B: Cyber security
Pack C: Wider implications of digital systems
Pack D: Planning and communication in digital systems

For more details on prices and discounts or to register your school:
visit **www.pgonline.co.uk**, email **sales@pgonline.co.uk**
or call **0845 840 0019.**